PORTFOLIO OF

PLANS FOR BUILT-IN & STORAGE PROJECTS

Augustus Suglia, A.I.A.

25 working drawings
for original designs
to build yourself

ARCO PUBLISHING, INC.
NEW YORK

The designs in this book were created and drawn by
Augustus Suglia, A.I.A., for a column entitled "Your
Home Plans" owned and syndicated by King Features,
235 East 45th Street, New York, NY 10017

Project Editor, Allen D. Bragdon
Designer, Vivian Chin

Published by Arco Publishing, Inc.
215 Park Avenue South, New York, NY 10003

Library of Congress Catalog Card Number: 83-71278
ISBN 0-668-05938-9 (Cloth Edition)
ISBN 0-668-05940-0 (Paper Edition)

Printed in the United States of America

10 9 8 7 6 5 4 3 2 1

Table of Contents

Introduction   4

WORKSPACES   5
   1. Carpenter's Bench   6
   2. Home Improvement Workcenter   9
   3. Student's Stereo & Storage   12
   4. Sewing Center   15
   5. Drop-down Hobby Table   18
   6. Home Office   21

BEDS & BENCHES   24
   7. Fold-up Back-to-Back Bunks   25
   8. Corner Beds   29
   9. Double-Decker Railroad   32
   10. Under-Seat Storage   35
   11. Living Wall with Seating   38

DESK & STOWAWAY UNITS   42
   12. Big Desk Space   43
   13. Home Management Center   46
   14. Paperwork Hideaway   50
   15. Open Bookcase Wall   53
   16. Cabinet Storage with Desk   56
   17. Modular Clothing Storage System   60

HOSPITALITY   64
   18. Hideaway Bar   65
   19. Dishes & Glasses Hutch   69
   20. Beverage-Service Duet   73
   21. Recreation Room Corner   77

FIREPLACES & WOODBINS   81
   22. Fieldstone with Double-Wall Firebox   82
   23. Contemporary Simplicity   85
   24. Colonial with Decorative Storage   88
   25. No-Masonry Prefab   91

Introduction

Architect Augustus Suglia selected 25 of his original project designs for this portfolio with these four criteria in mind: Each design makes the maximum practical use of the space it occupies. Its shape and dimensions are likely to fit the kinds of spaces in most homes that are not already planned for their maximum use. Although the dimensions can easily be changed to fit specific room-spaces, the dimensions given make maximum use of standard-sized materials for cost-efficiency. The skills and tools available to a moderately experienced, amateur, home carpenter are all that is required. Intricate cabinetry detailing and joining may be applied, of course, but even the moulding shapes, for example, are standard and readily available from stock.

Dimensions. The size of most of these projects can be changed by studying the dimensions given on the drawings and comparing those with the space available. Fireplaces, which are usually built in the center of a wall, for example, can be extended on either side of the firebox by continuing the masonry facing material as a veneer thickness built over the stud wall on each side. The shelf widths specified can also be extended but the shelves may sag betwen vertical supports if they run more than 30 inches. If greater uninterrupted length is desired, nail a ¾"x¾" vertical support at the face of the shelving and into the front edge of each shelf. Center these vertical face-supports between the vertical structural supports. If you nail through the back panel into the back edge of each shelf opposite the face-supports, no extra supporting members need to be attached to the back face of the shelves. When any changes in dimensions are made, don't forget also to change the Materials Lists provided with the drawings.

Materials. Except for large, flat surfaces the Materials Lists specify lumber in standard widths rather than plywood. All of the working drawings show dimensions for standard-size lumber as 1"x12" (which actually measures ¾"x11½" when you buy it). However, plywood is structurally stronger than most lumber, especially soft-woods. The large 4'x8' sheets in which plywood is sold can turn out to be less expensive than lumber per board foot. However, the labor component is higher. You will not only have to cut up the sheets into the dimensions of the lumber shown on the drawings, you will also have to tack and/or glue wood veneer edging or mounding strips onto the exposed edges of the plywood for a properly finished appearance. Especially for shelving applications, plywood's laminated construction makes it less subject than lumber to twisting, cupping and warping. For that reason, if you have experience working with plywood, it would be the superior material.

Door swings. When building a cabinet with doors, you may want to think about which direction they will swing open. If they protrude into a traffic lane, or will hit something, you may want to hang the hinges on the opposite side from the one shown in the working drawings.

Styling. By changing details and finishes the project can be made to blend with the period or other decorative style of the room it will live in. The simplest way to pick up a period look is to change the mouldings. They can have an amazing effect on the style of the piece. Lighting, and the style of the fixtures chosen, can also change the appearance of the piece without changing its dimensions. Lighting—spot or track—may be added to all the projects that have shelving or cabinets and you may be glad you did, especially if they are in a dark corner or have deep recesses.

A note about energy-efficient, prefab fireplaces.
These prefabricated metal fireboxes can be installed with "zero clearance" unless the instructions warn differently. This means that they are easy to install in any spot on an existing wall. It needs no masonry foundation and can be supported and surrounded with standard building materials, including combustible ones. Here is how these units work. Cool room air is drawn into the double-walled metal chamber-box, usually from vents on the bottom face of the facade. The cool air rises inside the heated chamber and warms as it flows upward. It then returns into the room through vents on the top face of the fireplace before it returns to the original room, heated sufficiently to maintain a comfortable temperature. The heated air can also be ducted to other rooms which can reduce demands on the primary furnace.

May you enjoy building and living with these projects.
The Editors

WORKSPACES

1.

CARPENTER'S BENCH
Work bench designed to provide good work and storage space

Find a corner in basement, garage or hobby room for a work bench designed to help the home handyman do his thing. Drawers at the side hold blueprints and other aids; cabinet above is for hand tools. Bins store nails within reach. Shelf at bottom houses heavy tools. There's a built-in standard vise assembly. Bench is 6 feet wide; 2 feet deep; 6 feet high.

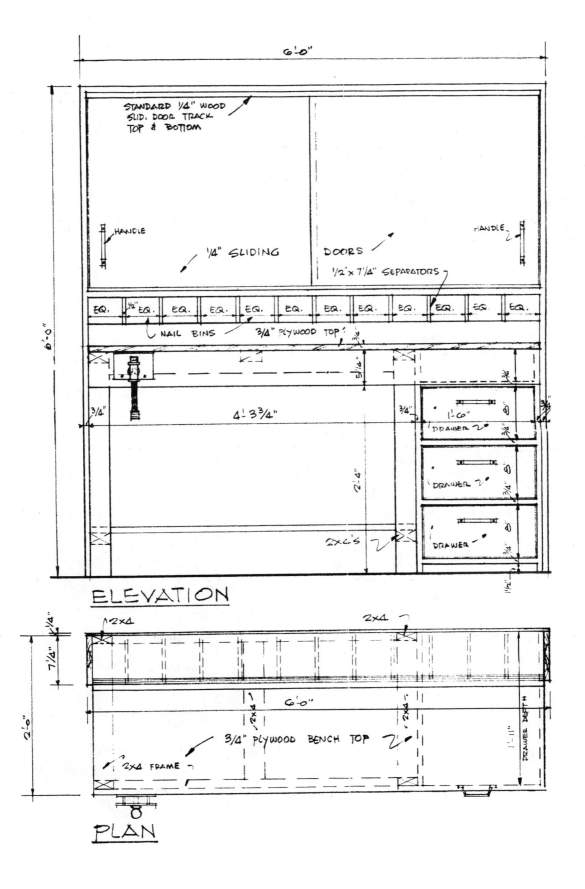

6'-0"

STANDARD 1/4" WOOD
SLID. DOOR TRACK
TOP & BOTTOM

HANDLE

1/4" SLIDING

DOORS

HANDLE

1/2" x 7 1/4" SEPARATORS

EQ. | 1/2" EQ. | EQ. | EQ. | EQ. | EQ. | EQ. | EQ. | EQ. | EQ. | EQ. | EQ.

NAIL BINS   3/4" PLYWOOD TOP   3/4"

6'-0"

3/4"

4'-3 3/4"

3/4"

1'-6"

DRAWER

2'-4"

DRAWER

2X4'S

DRAWER

ELEVATION

7 1/4"

2X4

2X4

2'-0"

6'-0"

3/4" PLYWOOD BENCH TOP

2X4

2X4

DRAWER DEPTH

1'-11"

2X4 FRAME

PLAN

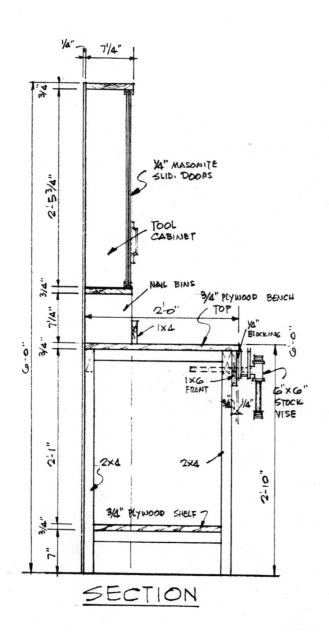

SECTION

MATERIAL LIST

24'	1"x8"	PINE	SHELVING
8'	1/2"x8"	"	FOR NAIL DIVIDERS
6'	1"x4"	"	NAIL BIN FRONT
30'	2"x4"		BENCH LEGS & FRAME
6'	1"x6"		BENCH FRONT

3/4"x4'x10' PLYWOOD } CUT FOR BENCH TOP
3/4"x2'x10' PLYWOOD } SHELF & DRAWERS
1/4"x4'x6' } MASONITE (PEGBOARD BACKING)
1/4"x2'x6' }
1/4"x2'-6"x6' MASONITE (SLID. DOORS)

5   DOOR & DRAWER HANDLES
2   6'-0" TOP & BOTTOM SLID. DOOR TRACKS

HOME IMPROVEMENT WORKCENTER

An easy-to-build workbench

A workman is only as good as his tools, and a home handyman only as effective as his work place. If his tools are scattered around the kitchen, if he has to clear floor space to spread out a project, he needs a workbench, such as this plan.

The bench is 4 feet wide. At each side, there's a 2-foot wide cabinet to store nails, tools, hardware, books. Cabinet under the workbench takes heavy-duty tools, paints, etc. Corkboard over bench is handy for pinning up plans for projects that are in process.

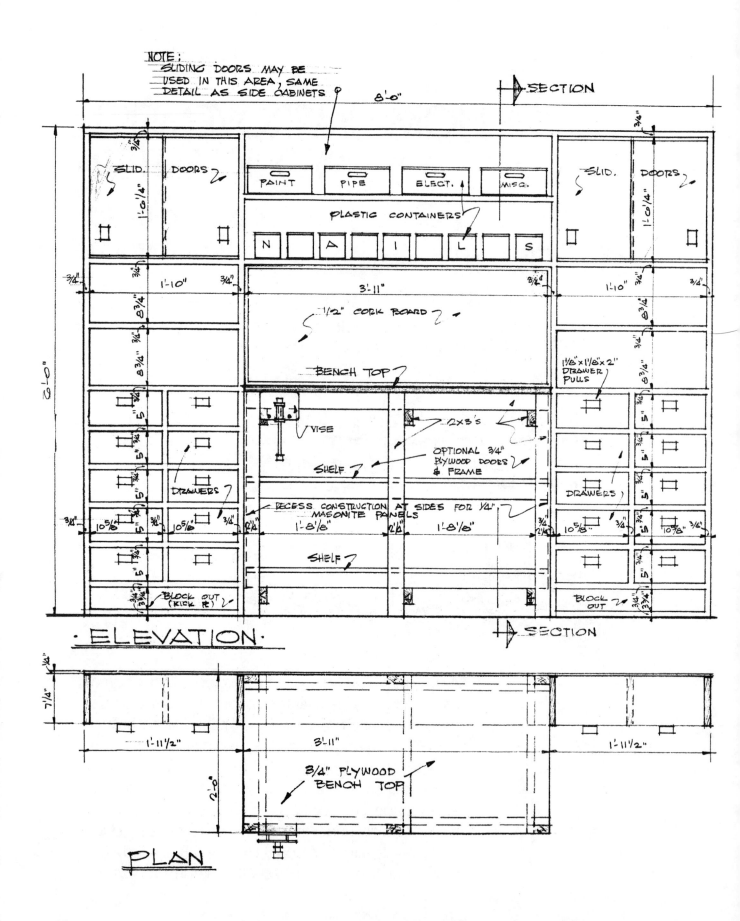

NOTE:
SLIDING DOORS MAY BE
USED IN THIS AREA, SAME
DETAIL AS SIDE CABINETS

SECTION

8'-0"

SLID. DOORS

1'-0 1/4"

PAINT   PIPE   ELECT.   MISC.

PLASTIC CONTAINERS

N A I L S

SLID. DOORS

1'-0 1/4"

3/4"   1'-10"   3/4"

8 3/4"

8 3/4"

1/2" CORK BOARD

3'-11"

BENCH TOP

3/4"   1'-10"   3/4"

8 3/4"

1 1/8" x 1 1/8" x 2"
DRAWER
PULLS

8 3/4"

VISE

2 x 3's

OPTIONAL 3/4"
PLYWOOD DOORS
& FRAME

SHELF

DRAWERS

5"   5"

5"   5"

DRAWERS

RECESS CONSTRUCTION AT SIDES FOR 1/4"
MASONITE PANELS

1'-8 1/8"   1'-8 1/8"

3/4"   10 5/8"   3/4"   10 5/8"   3/4"   2 1/4"   2 1/4"   3/4"   10 5/8"   3/4"   10 5/8"   3/4"

SHELF

BLOCK OUT
(KICK ?)

BLOCK OUT

2'-0"

· ELEVATION ·

SECTION

7 1/4"

1'-11 1/2"

3'-11"

3/4" PLYWOOD
BENCH TOP

1'-11 1/2"

2'-0"

PLAN

10

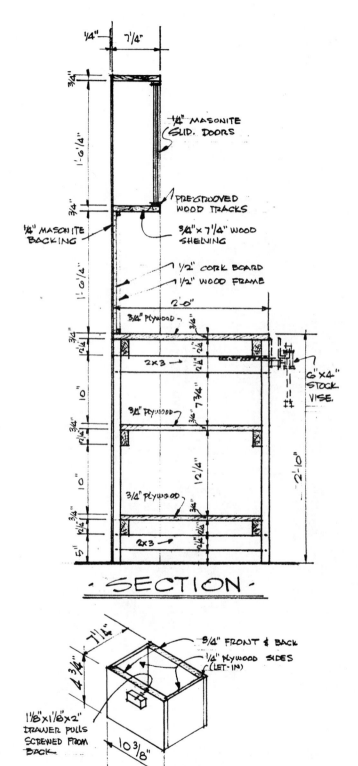

1/4" 7 1/4"

3/4"

1'-6 1/4"

1/4" MASONITE
SLID. DOORS

3/4"

1/4" MASONITE
BACKING

PRE-GROOVED
WOOD TRACKS

3/4" × 7 1/4" WOOD
SHELVING

1/2" CORK BOARD
1/2" WOOD FRAME

1'-6 1/4"

2'-0"

3/4" PLYWOOD

3/4"

2 1/4"

3/4"

2 1/4"

2×3

2 1/4"

6"×4"
STOCK
VISE.

3/4" 7 3/4"

3/4" PLYWOOD

0"

3/4"

0"

2'-0"

1 2 1/4"

3/4" PLYWOOD

3/4"

3/4"

1/4"

5"

2×3

2 1/4"

· SECTION ·

7 1/4"

3/4" FRONT & BACK
1/4" PLYWOOD SIDES
(LET-IN)

4 3/4"

1 1/8"×1 1/8"×2"
DRAWER PULLS
SCREWED FROM
BACK

10 3/8"

ISOMETRIC OF TYPICAL DRAWER

MATERIAL LIST

3/4" × 7 1/4" WOOD SHELVING -
81 LIN. FT.
2×3 - 54 LIN FT
(4) 1'-6" × 1'-0" × 1/4" MASONITE SLID. DOORS
(20) 3/4" × 10 3/8" × 4 3/4" DRAWER FRONT
(40) 1/4" × 6 3/4" × 4 1/2" DRAWER SIDES
(20) 1/4" × 7" × 10 3/8" DRAWER BOTTOMS
(20) 3/4" × 10 3/8" × 4 1/2" DRAWER BACK
(22) 1 1/8" × 1 1/8" × 2" DRAWER PULLS
(3) 2'-0" × 3'-11" × 3/4" PLYWOOD SHELVES
(2) 3 3/4" × 1'-10" × 3/4" BOTTOM KICK PLATE
(1) 3'-11" × 1'-6 1/4" × 1/2" CORK BOARD
    1/2" × 1/2"   11 LIN. FT.   " FRAME
    1 3/16" × 1/2" 4 LIN. FT. TOP PRE-GROOVED
                                TRACK
    1 3/16" × 1/4" 4 LIN. FT. BOTTOM PRE-
                                GROOVED TRACK
(2) 1/4" × 6'-0" MASONITE BACKING

WORK BENCH

3.

STUDENT'S STEREO & STORAGE

This unit works well as a teen-ager's homework haven and clutter-catcher

Here's a storage unit that is useful in a family room or bedroom. There's a drop desk at center and, around it, shelves for books, record albums, stereo and speakers. Drawers file paper, clips and other supplies. Built of standard-size wood shelving, unit has 4x6 pre-finished wood panel at back. It is 4 feet ½ inch wide, 11½ inches deep, 6 feet high.

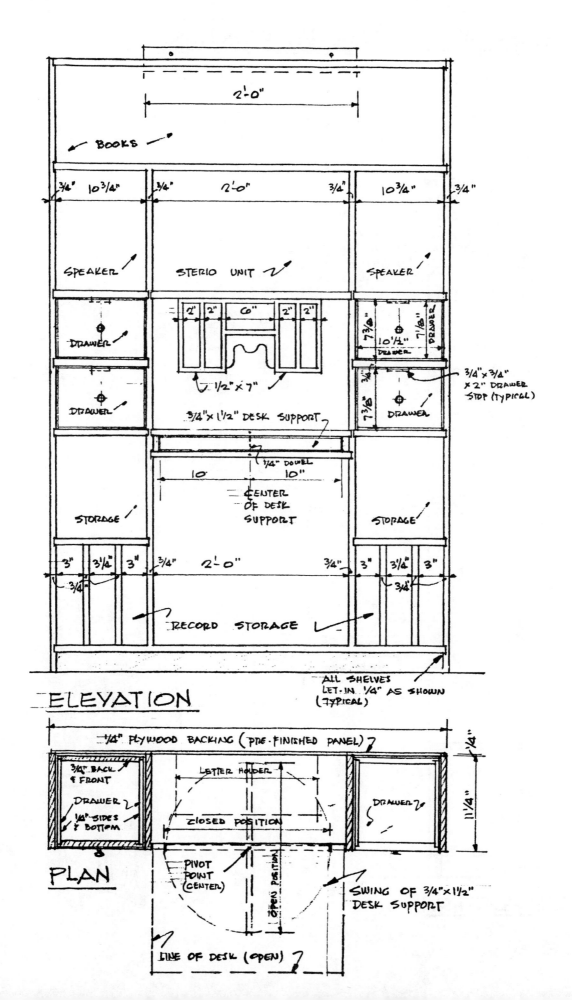

2'-0"

BOOKS

3/4" 10 3/4" 3/4" **2'-0"** 3/4" 10 3/4" 3/4"

SPEAKER   STERIO UNIT   SPEAKER

2" 2" 6" 2" 2"

7 3/8"   7/8"   DRAWER

DRAWER   10 1/2"   DRAWER

1/2" x 7"

3/4" x 3/4"
x 2" DRAWER
STOP (TYPICAL)

DRAWER   7 3/8"   7/8"

7 3/8"   DRAWER

3/4" x 1 1/2" DESK SUPPORT

1/4" DOWEL

10   10"

CENTER
OF DESK
SUPPORT

STORAGE   STORAGE

3" 3 1/4" 3" 3/4" **2'-0"** 3/4" 3" 3 1/4" 3"

3/4"   3/4"

RECORD STORAGE

ALL SHELVES
LET·IN 1/4" AS SHOWN
(TYPICAL)

ELEVATION

1/4" PLYWOOD BACKING (PRE·FINISHED PANEL)   1/4"

3/4" BACK
& FRONT

LETTER HOLDER

11 1/4"

DRAWER

1/4" SIDES
& BOTTOM

CLOSED POSITION

DRAWER

PLAN

PIVOT
POINT
(CENTER)

OPEN POSITION

SWING OF 3/4" x 1 1/2"
DESK SUPPORT

LINE OF DESK (OPEN)

13

DESK & STORAGE CENTER

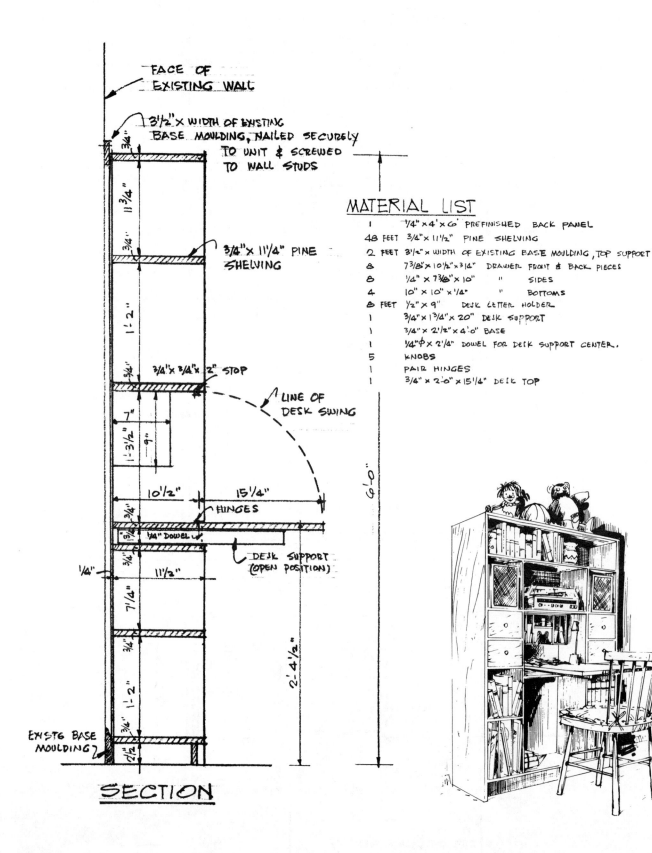

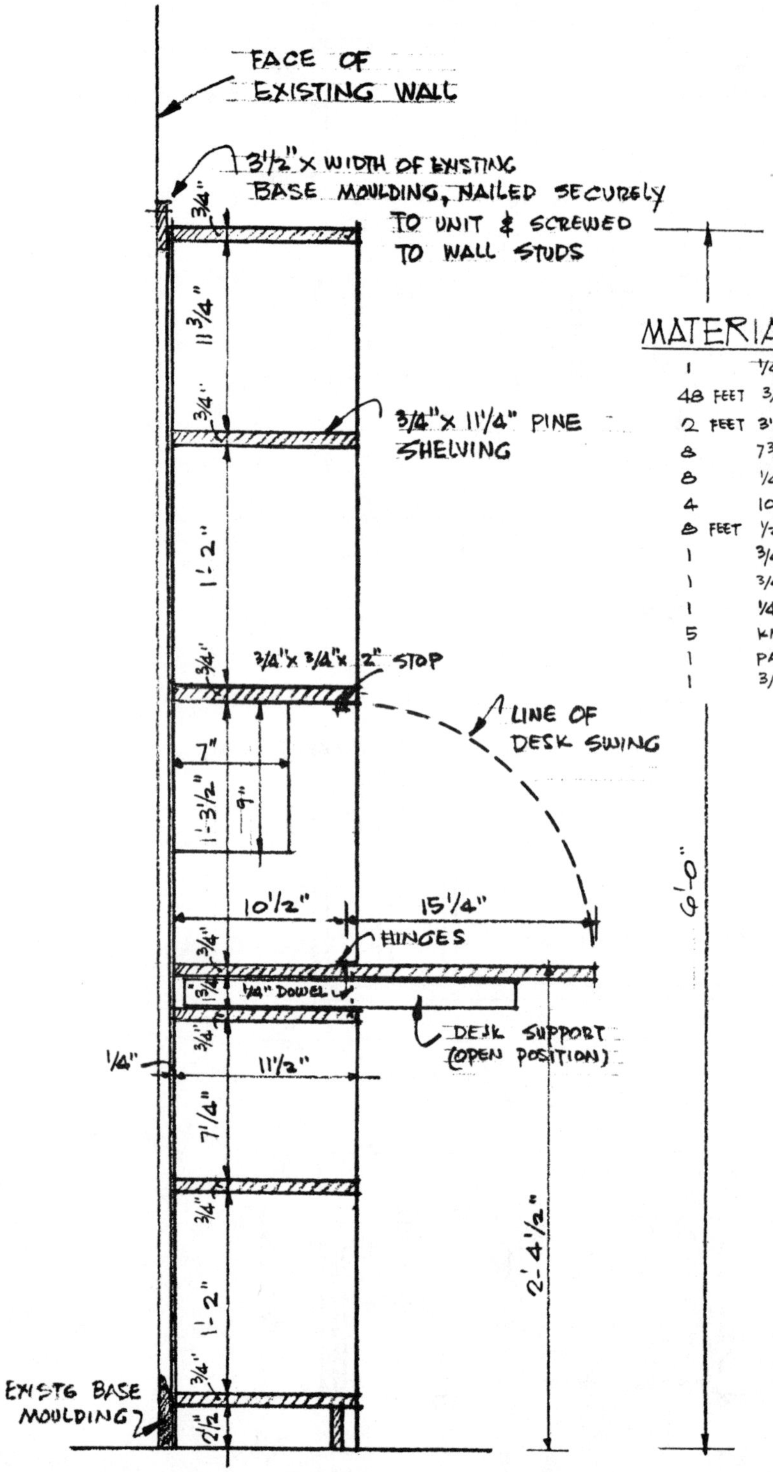
FACE OF EXISTING WALL
3½" x WIDTH OF EXISTING BASE MOULDING, NAILED SECURELY TO UNIT & SCREWED TO WALL STUDS
3/4"
11 3/4"
3/4"
3/4" x 11¼" PINE SHELVING
1'-2"
3/4"
3/4" x 3/4" x 2" STOP
LINE OF DESK SWING
7"
1'-3½"
9"
10½"
15¼"
3/4"
HINGES
1¾"
¼" DOWEL
DESK SUPPORT (OPEN POSITION)
¼"
3/4"
11½"
7¼"
3/4"
1'-2"
3/4"
2½"
EXIST'G BASE MOULDING
2'-4½"
6'-0"

SECTION

MATERIAL LIST

1		¼" x 4' x 6' PREFINISHED BACK PANEL
48	FEET	3/4" x 11½" PINE SHELVING
2	FEET	3½" x WIDTH OF EXISTING BASE MOULDING, TOP SUPPORT
8		7 3/8" x 10½" x 3/4" DRAWER FRONT & BACK PIECES
8		¼" x 7 3/8" x 10" " SIDES
4		10" x 10" x ¼" " BOTTOMS
8	FEET	½" x 9" DESK LETTER HOLDER
1		3/4" x 1 3/4" x 20" DESK SUPPORT
1		3/4" x 2½" x 4'-0" BASE
1		¼" φ x 2¼" DOWEL FOR DESK SUPPORT CENTER.
5		KNOBS
1		PAIR HINGES
1		3/4" x 2'-0" x 15¼" DESK TOP

SEWING CENTER
Features handy fold-down table

This sewing center can be built into a corner or free-standing. The table folds up and hides behind louvered doors when it's not in use. Shelves store sewing supplies and linens. The sewing center is 5 feet, 4 inches wide; 15½ inches deep; room height.

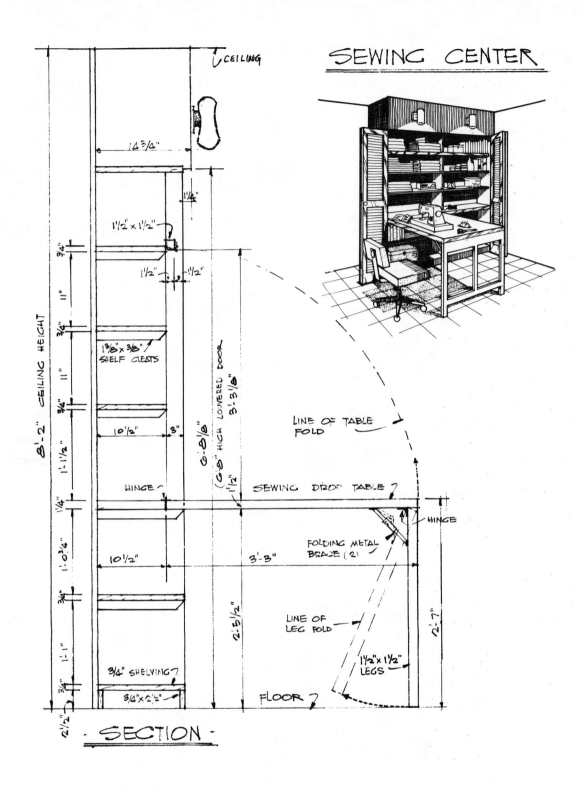

SEWING CENTER

CEILING

14 3/4"

1 1/4"

1 1/2" x 1 1/2"

1 1/2"   1 1/2"

3/4"

11"

3/4"

1 3/8" x 3/8"
SHELF CLEATS

11"

3/4"

10 1/2"   3"

1-1 1/2"

8'-2" CEILING HEIGHT

6'-8 1/8"

(6'-8" HIGH LOUVERED DOOR)

3'-3 1/8"

LINE OF TABLE
FOLD

HINGE

1 1/2"

SEWING DROP TABLE

HINGE

1/4"

FOLDING METAL
BRACE (2)

1-0 3/4"

10 1/2"

3'-3"

2'-5 1/2"

2'-7"

3/4"

LINE OF
LEG FOLD

1-1"

3/4" SHELVING

1 1/2" x 1 1/2"
LEGS

3/4" x 2 1/2"

FLOOR

2 1/2"

- SECTION -

MATERIAL LIST

4	SHEETS	3/4" x 4' x 8' PLYWOOD
20	FEET	3/8" x 1 3/8" SHELF CLEATS
11	FEET	3/4" x 2 1/2" BASE
18	FEET	1 1/2" x 1 1/2" TABLE END & TOP BAR
1		1 1/2" x 5'-4" SHELF
1		2'-8 1/2" x 3'-3" DROP TABLE
4		16" BI-FOLD DOORS
6	PAIR	CONCEALED HINGES
2		FOLDING METAL BRACES
2		BUTTERFLY CATCHES
2		DOOR KNOBS

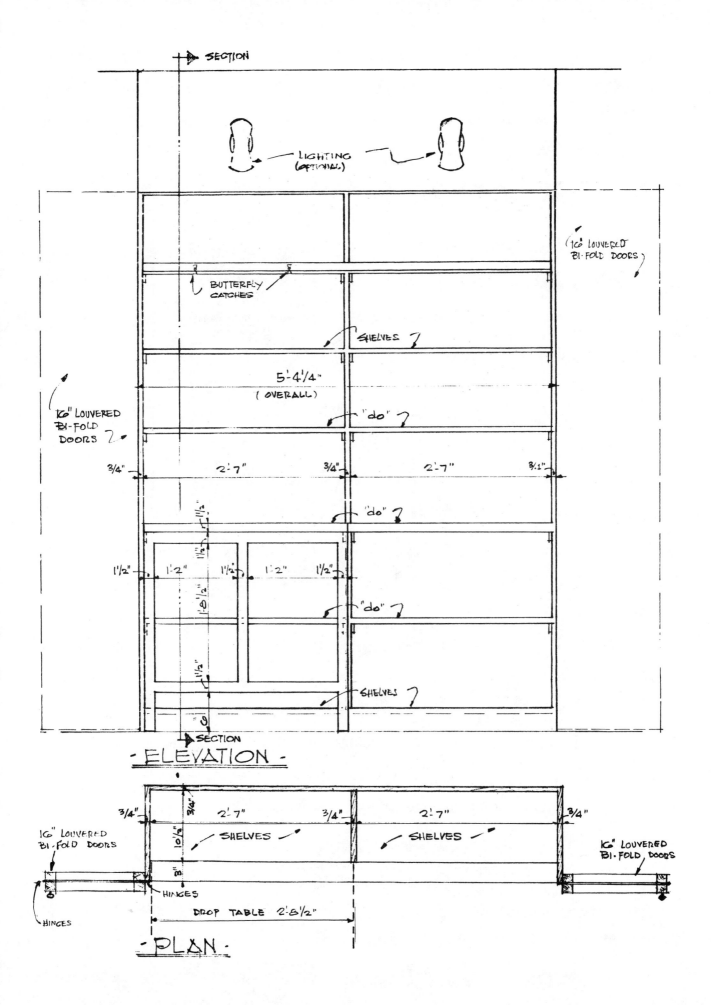

SECTION

LIGHTING
(OPTIONAL)

(16" LOUVERED
BI-FOLD DOORS)

BUTTERFLY
CATCHES

SHELVES

5'-4¼"
(OVERALL)

"do"

16" LOUVERED
BI-FOLD
DOORS

3/4"   2'-7"   3/4"   2'-7"   3/4"

"do"

1½"

1½"   1'-2"   1½"   1'-2"   1½"

1'-0½"

"do"

1½"

SHELVES

SECTION

- ELEVATION -

3/4"   2'-7"   3/4"   2'-7"   3/4"

3/4"

16" LOUVERED
BI-FOLD DOORS

SHELVES   SHELVES

10½"

3"

16" LOUVERED
BI-FOLD DOORS

HINGES

HINGES

DROP TABLE 2'-8½"

- PLAN -

17

5.

DROP-DOWN HOBBY TABLE

Now you see it, now you don't

If space is at a premium in your home or apartment, consider such space-saving designs as fold-down furniture. This hobby table is a good example. When you need it, it folds down. When you don't, it folds up. The support, with its framed bulletin board, folds flat against the table, completely disguising its function.

Note shelves above for storing games, books, whatever. Below, sliding door cabinets provide more stowaway space. Ideal for a child's room, hobby room or family room, the unit could serve as a kitchen snack bar. It is 2 feet, 9½ inches wide; 9½ inches deep, closed; 3 feet, 9½ inches deep open; 5 feet, 8¼ inches high.

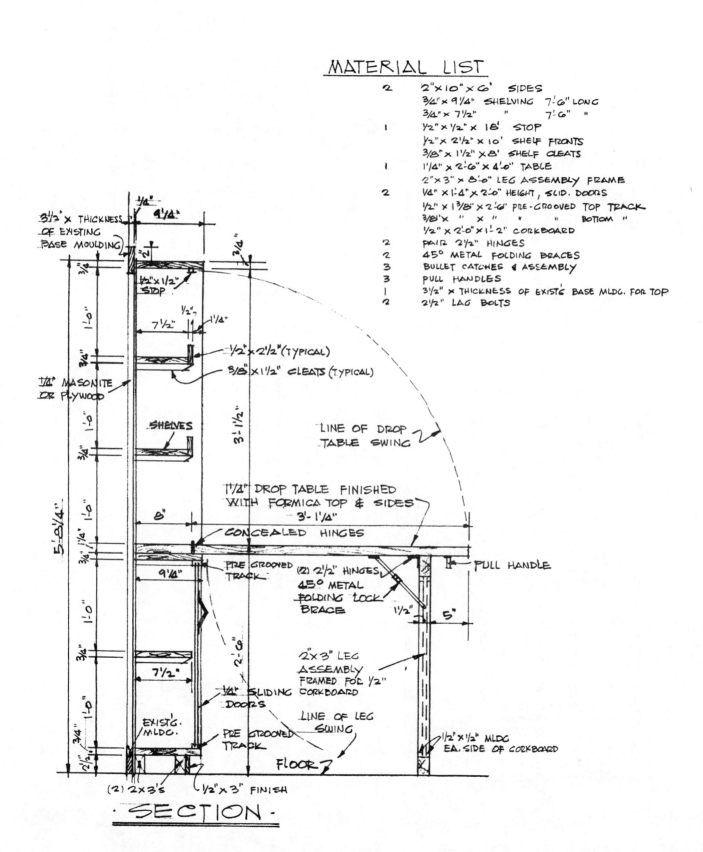

MATERIAL LIST

2	2" x 10" x 6' SIDES
	3/4" x 9 1/4" SHELVING 7'-6" LONG
	3/4" x 7 1/2" " 7'-6" "
1	1/2" x 1/2" x 18' STOP
	1/2" x 2 1/2" x 10' SHELF FRONTS
	3/8" x 1 1/2" x 8' SHELF CLEATS
1	1 1/4" x 2'-6" x 4'-0" TABLE
	2" x 3" x 8'-0" LEG ASSEMBLY FRAME
2	1/4" x 1'-4" x 2'-0" HEIGHT, SLID. DOORS
	1/2" x 1 3/8" x 2'-6" PRE-GROOVED TOP TRACK
	3/8" x " x " " " BOTTOM "
	1/2" x 2'-0" x 1'-2" CORKBOARD
2	PAIR 2 1/2" HINGES
2	45° METAL FOLDING BRACES
3	BULLET CATCHES & ASSEMBLY
3	PULL HANDLES
1	3 1/2" x THICKNESS OF EXIST'G BASE MLDG. FOR TOP
2	2 1/2" LAG BOLTS

3 1/2" x THICKNESS OF EXISTING BASE MOULDING

1/2" x 1/2" STOP

1/4" MASONITE OR PLYWOOD

1/2" x 2 1/2" (TYPICAL)

3/8" x 1 1/2" CLEATS (TYPICAL)

SHELVES

LINE OF DROP TABLE SWING

1 1/4" DROP TABLE FINISHED WITH FORMICA TOP & SIDES — 3'-1 1/4"

CONCEALED HINGES

PRE GROOVED TRACK

(2) 2 1/2" HINGES

45° METAL FOLDING LOCK BRACE

PULL HANDLE

2" x 3" LEG ASSEMBLY FRAMED FOR 1/2" CORKBOARD

1/4" SLIDING DOORS

LINE OF LEG SWING

EXIST'G. MLDG.

PRE GROOVED TRACK

FLOOR

1/2" x 1/2" MLDG EA. SIDE OF CORKBOARD

(2) 2x3's

1/2" x 3" FINISH

· SECTION ·

HOBBY DROP TABLE & STORAGE

Elevation

2'-6½"

1½"   1½"

2½" LAG BOLTS TO WALL STUDS

THREE BULLET CATCHES

SHELF

3/8" x 1½" CLEATS
(TYPICAL)

SHELF

DROP TABLE

SUNKEN
BULLET CATCHES

DOOR
PULLS

½" CORKBOARD

SLID.
DOOR

SLID.
DOOR

6¼"   1'-6"   6¼"

- ELEVATION -

Plan

1½"   2'-6½"   1½"

¼"

9¼"   2x10   6"   SHELVES   2x10

2"x10"   2"x10"

2'-6"

DROP TABLE

3'-11¼"

LEG ASSEMBLY

- PLAN -

HOME OFFICE
Work center has ample storage space

As home bookkeeping accumulates, including everything from store lists to tax returns, one thing becomes obvious: Every home needs a home office. Here's one you can build yourself. It includes a desk, mail bins, shelves and a roomy lower cabinet. Unit's 4 feet wide; bookcase 9¼ inches deep; desk 13¼ inches deep; height's adjustable.

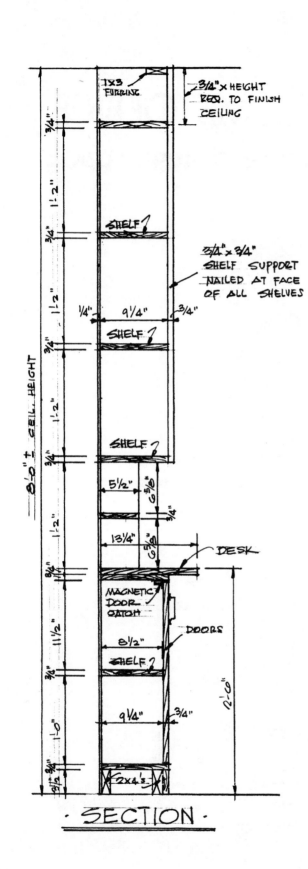

· SECTION ·

MATERIAL LIST

37	LIN. FT.	3/4" × 9 1/4" SHELVING & SIDES
4	LIN. FT.	3/4" × 3/4" FRONT CENTER SUPPORT
7	LIN. FT.	3/4" × 5 1/2" MAIL BIN
4	LIN. FT.	3/4" × 13 1/4" DESK
1	PLYWOOD	3/4" × 2'-0" × 2'-0" DOORS (CUT TO FIT)
4	LIN. FT.	1 1/2" × 2 1/2" (2×4) BASE
2	LIN. FT.	3/4" × 3 1/2" BASE FRONT
2	PAIR	2 1/2" CONCEALED HINGES
2		METAL DOOR PULLS
2		MAGNETIC CATCHES
4	LIN. FT.	1" × 3" FURRING (AT CEIL.)
4	LIN. FT.	3/4" × HEIGHT REQ. (TOP OF UNIT TO CEIL.)
1		1/4" × 4'-0" × 8'-0" PRE FINISHED BACK PANEL

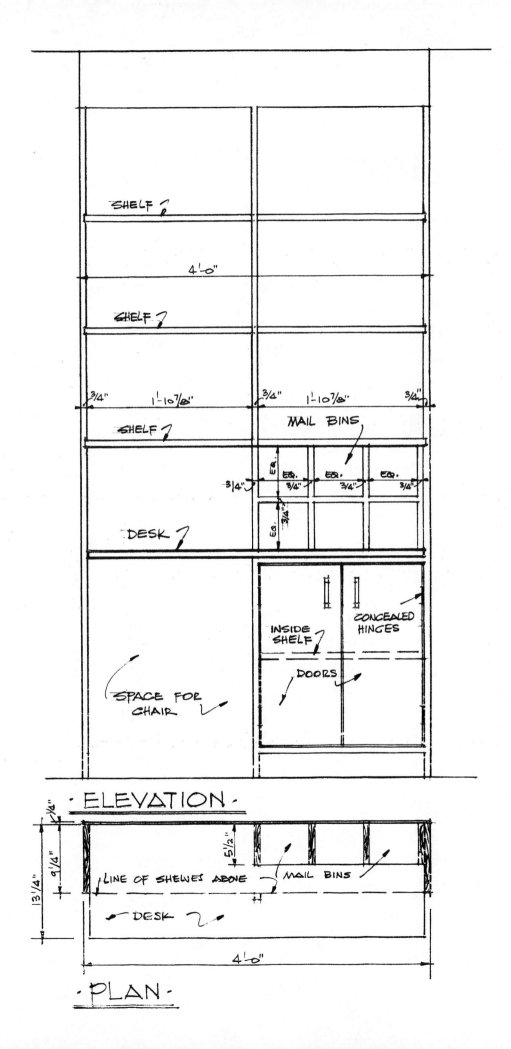

SHELF

4'-0"

SHELF

3/4"   1'-10⅞"   3/4"   1'-10⅞"   3/4"

SHELF

MAIL BINS

EQ.

3/4"   EQ.   EQ.   EQ.
3/4"   3/4"   3/4"

3/4"

DESK

EQ.

INSIDE
SHELF

CONCEALED
HINGES

SPACE FOR
CHAIR

DOORS

· ELEVATION ·

1/4"

9/4"

5½"

13/4"

LINE OF SHELVES ABOVE

MAIL BINS

DESK

4'-0"

· PLAN ·

BEDS & BENCHES

7.

FOLD-UP BACK-TO-BACK BUNKS
Space-savers for children's room

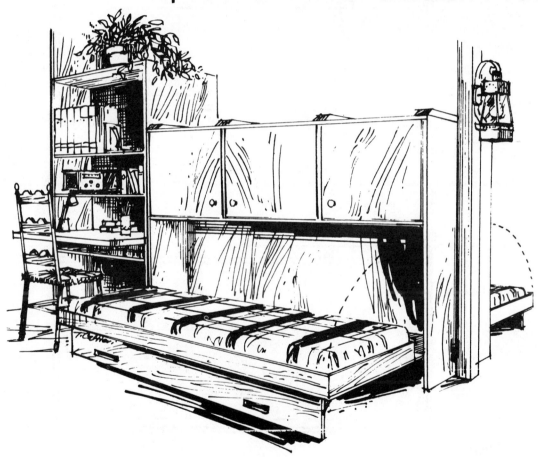

Build this foldaway bunk bed as a single unit against a wall or, as pictured, as a double unit with a partition that provides privacy and a desk and bunk on each side. When not in use, the bunks fold up under top storage cabinets, leaving floor space free for play.

The unit is 8 feet, 10¾ inches long; 3 feet, 10¼ inches wide for one unit; 7 feet, 8¾ inches wide for two units. Desk section is 7 feet high; bunk bed section is 6 feet high.

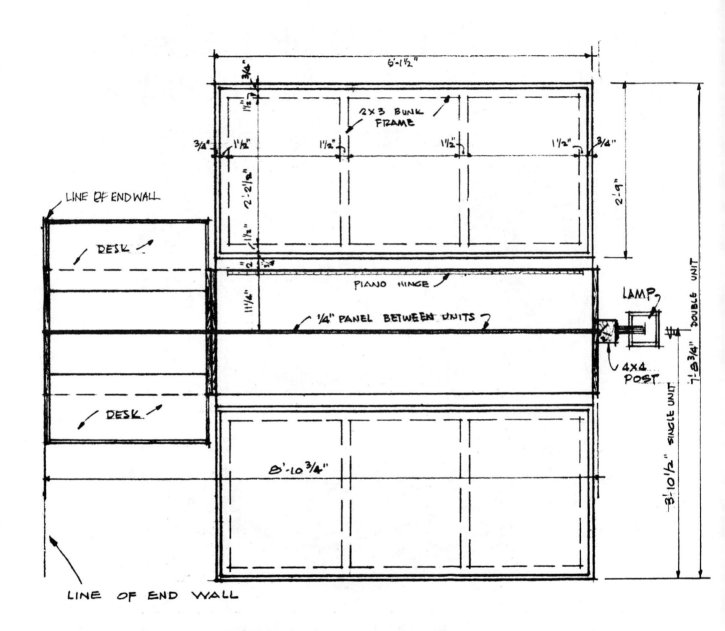

6'-1½"

¾"

1½"

2X3 BUNK FRAME

3/4" 1½" 1½" 1½" 1½" 3/4"

2'-9"

LINE OF END WALL

DESK

2'-2⅛"

1½"

¾"

½"

PIANO HINGE

1¼"

LAMP

DOUBLE UNIT 7'-8¾"

¼" PANEL BETWEEN UNITS

4X4 POST

DESK

8'-10¾" SINGLE UNIT

8'-10¾"

LINE OF END WALL

PLAN

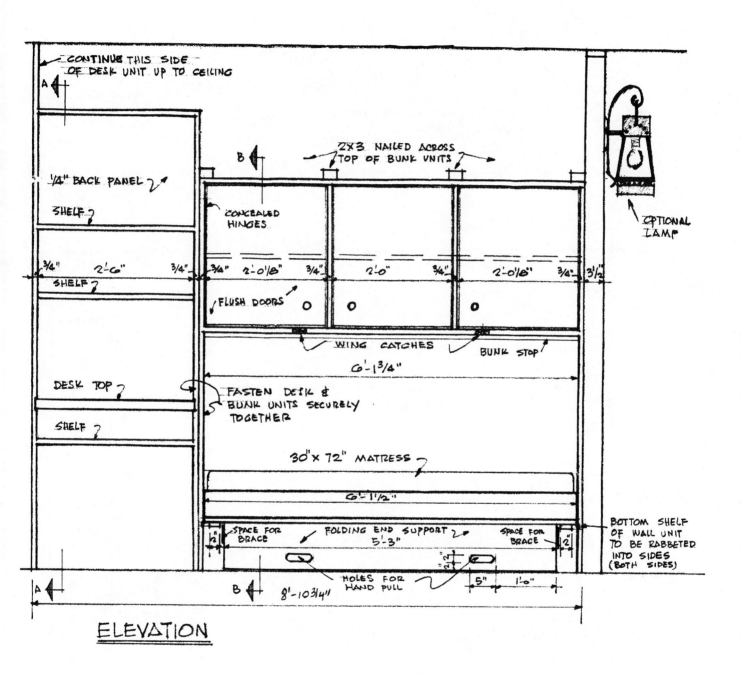

CONTINUE THIS SIDE OF DESK UNIT UP TO CEILING

A

1/4" BACK PANEL

SHELF

3/4" 2'-6" 3/4"

SHELF

DESK TOP

SHELF

B

2X3 NAILED ACROSS TOP OF BUNK UNITS

CONCEALED HINGES

3/4" 2'-0 1/8" 3/4"   2'-0"   3/4" 2'-0 1/8" 3/4" 3 1/2"

FLUSH DOORS   O   O   O

WING CATCHES   BUNK STOP

6'-1 3/4"

FASTEN DESK & BUNK UNITS SECURELY TOGETHER

30" X 72" MATTRESS

6'-1 1/2"

SPACE FOR BRACE   FOLDING END SUPPORT   SPACE FOR BRACE
1/2"   5'-3"   2"

HOLES FOR HAND PULL   2 1/2" 5" 1'-0"

A   B   8'-10 3/4"

OPTIONAL LAMP

BOTTOM SHELF OF WALL UNIT TO BE RABBETED INTO SIDES (BOTH SIDES)

ELEVATION

MATERIAL LIST

NOTE: DIVIDE MATERIAL LIST IN HALF FOR SINGLE UNIT.

Qty		Description
90 LIN. FT.		3/4" x 11 1/4" (1 x 12) PINE SHELVING
2	4x8	3/4" PLYWOOD
1		2"x4"x1'-4" CEIL. SUPPORT
1	POST	4"x4"x CEIL. HEIGHT
32 LIN. FT.		2"x3"
2		3/4"x7 1/4"x5'-0" DESK SHELF (ABOVE DESK)
2		1/4"x1 1/2"x4'-6" " MOULDING
2	3x6	3/4" PLYWOOD DOORS
2		1/2"x2'-6"x6'-0" PLYWOOD (UNDER MATRESS)
36 LIN. FT.		3/4"x5 1/2" BUNK BED FRAME
2		3/4"x8"x5'-3" FOLDING END SUPPORT (END OF BUNK)
1		1/4"x2'-7 1/2"x7'-0" DESK BACK PANEL
1		1/4"x6'-2 1/4"x6'-0" BUNK BACK PANEL
1		1"x2"x8'-0" DESK CLEAT & ENDS FOR FOLDING SUPPORT
2		3/4"x7 1/4"x12'-4" BOTTOM OF BUNK CAB.
6	PAIR	HINGES (CONCEAL TYPE)
6		KNOBS
4		PIANO HINGES (5'-0" LONG)
4		WING CATCHES
2		3/4"x5"x6'-1 3/4" BUNK STOPS

FOLD-AWAY BUNK BEDS

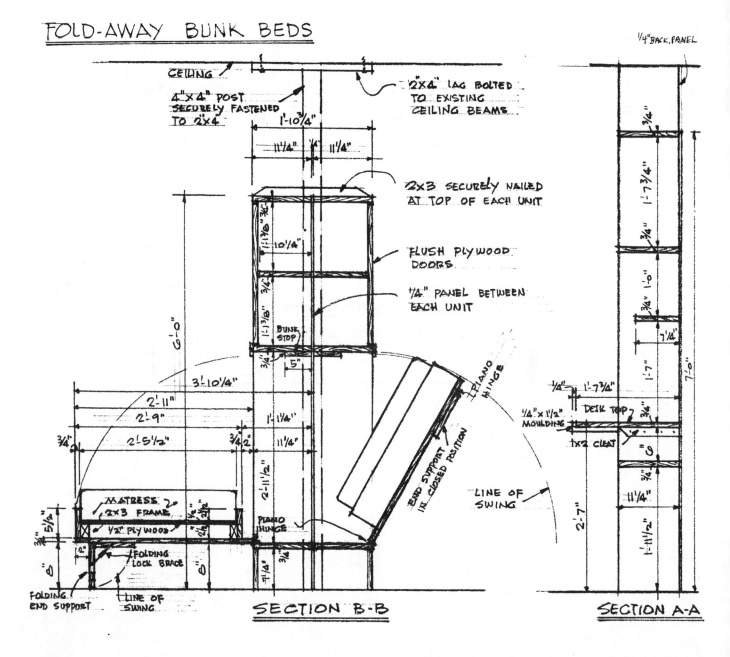

SECTION B-B

SECTION A-A

CORNER BEDS
Space-saving plan for a small bedroom

You can sleep two in a small bedroom if you build this corner arrangement of bunk beds. Including the table that separates them, each projects 8 feet, 9¾ inches from the corner, leaving floor space free for child's play.

Pull-out drawers are built under each bunk. Use them to store linens or clothing. Cabinets over each unit can stow toys, games, etc. Corner table is handy for lamp, radio and clock.

Units can be stained or painted as you prefer.

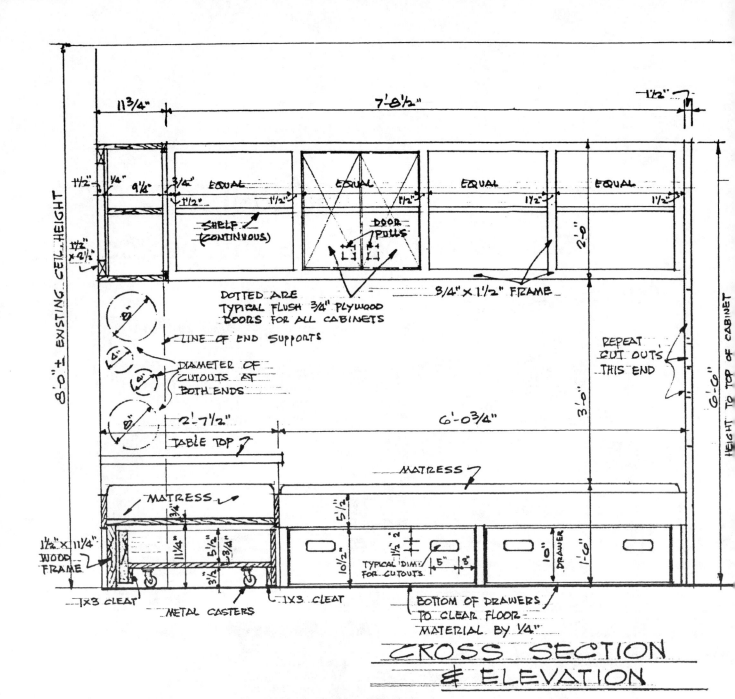

11 3/4" 7'-8 1/2" 1/2"

8'-0" ± EXISTING CEIL. HEIGHT

1 1/2" 1/4" 9 1/8" 3/4" EQUAL EQUAL EQUAL EQUAL

1 1/2" 1 1/2" 1 1/2" 1 1/2" 1 1/2"

SHELF (CONTINUOUS)

DOOR PULLS

2'-0"

3/4" x 1 1/2" FRAME

DOTTED ARE TYPICAL FLUSH 3/4" PLYWOOD DOORS FOR ALL CABINETS

LINE OF END SUPPORTS

DIAMETER OF CUTOUTS AT BOTH ENDS

8" 4" 4" 8"

REPEAT CUT OUTS THIS END

3'-0"

6'-6" HEIGHT TO TOP OF CABINET

2'-7 1/2" 6'-0 3/4"

TABLE TOP

MATRESS

MATRESS

3/4"

11 1/4" 5 1/2" 3/4"

5 1/2"

10 1/2" 1 1/2" 1 1/2"

TYPICAL DIM FOR CUTOUTS 5" 3"

10" DRAWER 1'-0"

1 1/2" x 11 1/4" WOOD FRAME

3 1/2"

1x3 CLEAT

METAL CASTERS

1x3 CLEAT

BOTTOM OF DRAWERS TO CLEAR FLOOR MATERIAL BY 1/4"

CROSS SECTION & ELEVATION

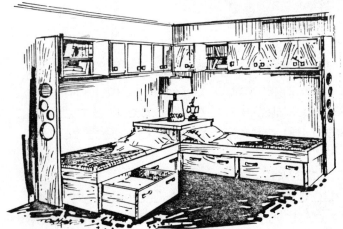

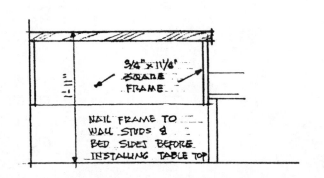

3/4" x 11 1/8" SQUARE FRAME

NAIL FRAME TO WALL STUDS & BED SIDES BEFORE INSTALLING TABLE TOP

TABLE SECTION

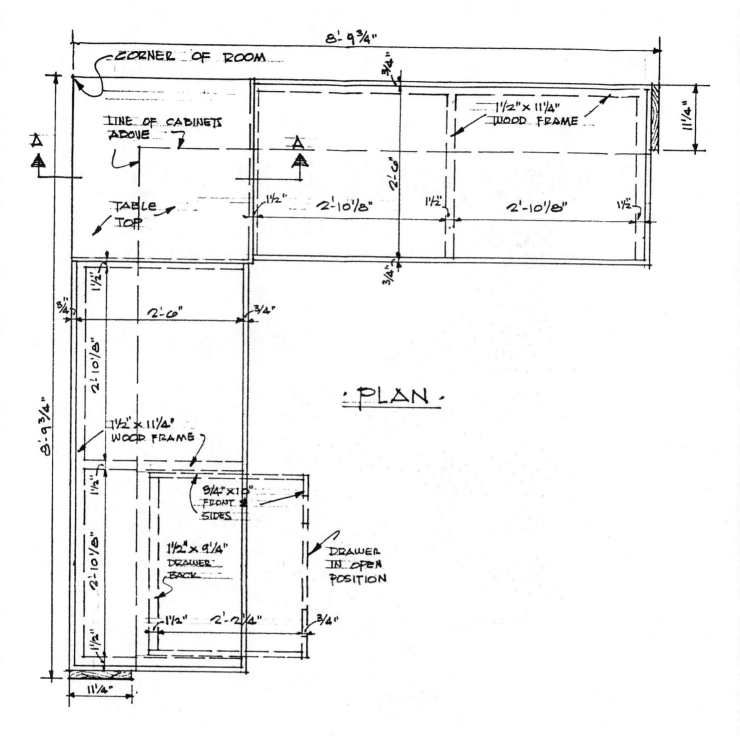

8'-9¾"

CORNER OF ROOM

3/4"

1½" × 11¼"
WOOD FRAME

11¼"

LINE OF CABINETS
ABOVE

A

TABLE
TOP

1½" 2'-10⅛" 1½" 2'-10⅛" 1½"

2'-0"

3/4"

· PLAN ·

8'-9¾"

3/4" 2'-0" 3/4"

1½"

2'-10⅛"

1½" × 11¼"
WOOD FRAME

3/4" × 10"
FRONT &
SIDES

1½" × 9¼"
DRAWER
BACK

DRAWER
IN OPEN
POSITION

2'-10⅛"

1½" 2'-2¼" 3/4"

1½"

11¼"

MATERIAL LIST·

2		1½" × 11¼" × 6'-6"	VERTICAL ENDS WITH CUTOUTS
27	LIN.FT.	1½" × 11¼"	BUNK BED FRAME
17	" "	3/4" × 5½"	" " MATRESS FRAME
2		3/4" × 2'-6" × 6'-0"	" " " BOARD (PLYWOOD)
2		3/4" × 10" × 32'	" " DRAWER FRONT & SIDES
2		3/4" × 2'-2¼" × 6'-0"	" " " BOTTOM
4		3/4" × 2½" × 6'-0"	" " " CLEATS
1		1⅛" × 2'-7½" × 2'-7½"	TABLE TOP
1		3/4" × 11¼" × 11'	" FRAME
44	LIN.FT.	3/4" × 11¼"	TOP CABINET TOP & SIDES
18	LIN.FT.	3/4" × 9¼"	" " CENTER SHELF.
2		¼" × 2'-0" × 18'	" " BACK PANEL
4		1½" × 2½" × 36'	" " BACK FRAME
52	LIN.FT.	3/4" × 1½"	" " FRONT FRAME
2		3/4" × 2'-0" × 8'-0"	" " DOORS
16		CASTERS	
16	PAIR	FLUSH HINGES	

31

DOUBLE-DECKER RAILROAD
The metal railings and ladder also look authentic if made of varnished oak

If Dad builds this caboose-style bunk bed for the boys, you won't have to nag them at bedtime. They'll actually look forward to chugging off to sleep Pullman style, although there's likely to be some discussion about who gets to climb the ladder that leads to the upper berth.

Upper bunk is designed with a railing that will keep a restless sleeper safely aboard. Lower bunk is designed with openings that simulate old-fashioned train windows.

Paint the caboose a bright color, using a stencil to letter in the railroad's name. Caboose is 8'5″ long; 3'2″ wide; 5'4″ high.

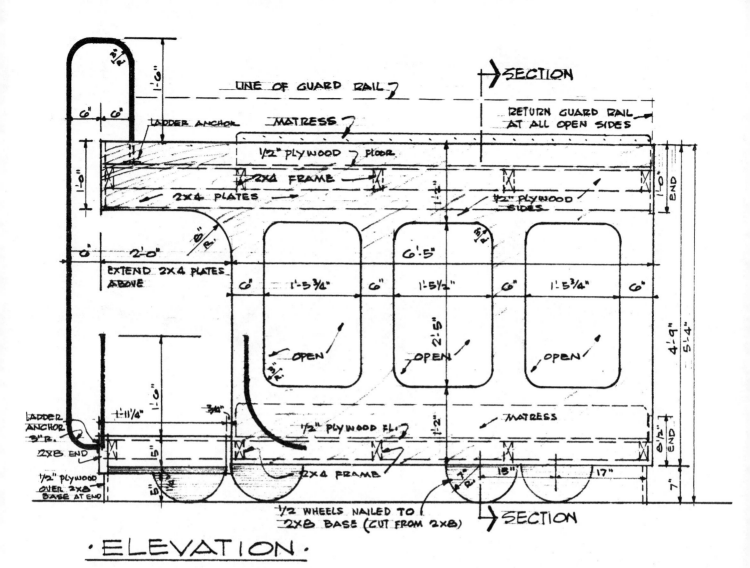

SECTION

LINE OF GUARD RAIL

RETURN GUARD RAIL AT ALL OPEN SIDES

LADDER ANCHOR   MATRESS

1/2" PLYWOOD FLOOR

2X4 FRAME

2X4 PLATES   1/2" PLYWOOD SIDES

EXTEND 2X4 PLATES ABOVE

OPEN   6'-5"   OPEN   OPEN

2'-5"

LADDER ANCHOR
3"R.
2X8 END
1/2" PLYWOOD OVER 2X8 BASE AT END

1/2" PLYWOOD FL.

MATRESS

2X4 FRAME

1/2 WHEELS NAILED TO 2X8 BASE (CUT FROM 2X8)

15"   17"

SECTION

· ELEVATION ·

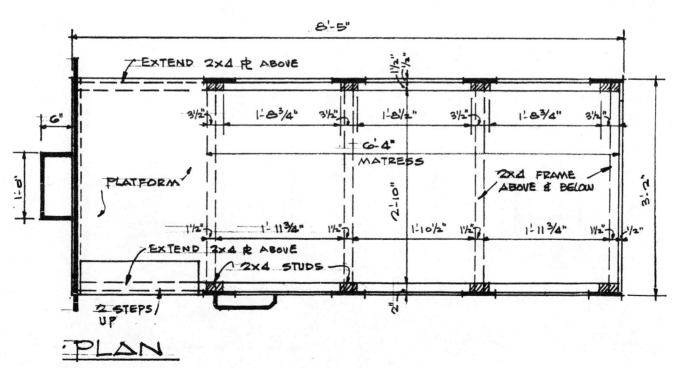

8'-5"

EXTEND 2X4 PL ABOVE

1'-8 3/4"   3 1/2"   1'-8 1/2"   3 1/2"   1'-8 3/4"   3 1/2"

6'-4"
MATRESS

PLATFORM

2X4 FRAME ABOVE & BELOW

1'-11 3/4"   1 1/2"   1'-10 1/2"   1 1/2"   1'-11 3/4"   1 1/2"

2'-10"

3'-2"

EXTEND 2X4 PL ABOVE

2X4 STUDS

2 STEPS UP

PLAN

CABOOSE BUNK BEDS

MATERIAL LIST

2	SHEETS	1/2" × 3'-2" × 10'
2	SHEETS	1/2" × 4' × 7'
76	LIN. FT.	2×4 (1 1/2" × 3 1/2" ACTUAL SIZE)
25	" "	2×8 (1 1/2" × 7 1/4" " ")-
2	" "	5/4" × 6" (1 1/4" × 5 1/4" STEP)

1/2"⌀ PIPE RAILINGS AND LADDER

NOTE: ENTIRE FRAME SHOULD BE
ASSEMBLED WITH 1/4" BOLT & NUT
CONSTRUCTION FOR STRONGEST JOINTS.
PLYWOOD MAY THEN BE ADDED WITH
FINISHING NAILS, COUNTER SINK
NAIL HEADS APPROX. 1/8" AND FILL
IN WITH PLASTIC WOOD TYPE COMPOUND.
WHEN COMPLETE SAND & PAINT.

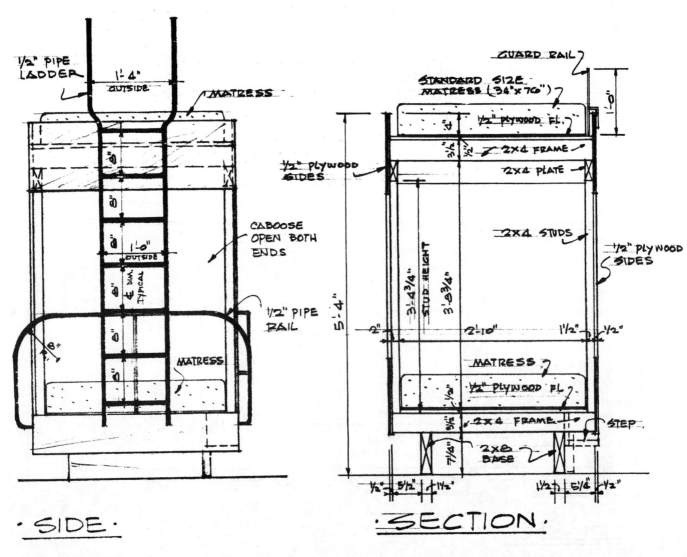

· SIDE ·   · SECTION ·

10.

UNDER-SEAT STORAGE

Corner Seating Unit Has Box Construction

Why buy furniture when it can be as economical and easy to build as these corner benches?

The base of each bench is a simple-to-construct plywood box with a hinged top that opens on a bonus of storage space. A corner table, designed to hold a reading lamp, is built-in. Make removable cushions with foam to cover seat and back of each bench. You can paint or stain the plywood, as you prefer. The unit projects 8 feet from the corner on each side. It is 21¼ inches deep; height, 32 inches.

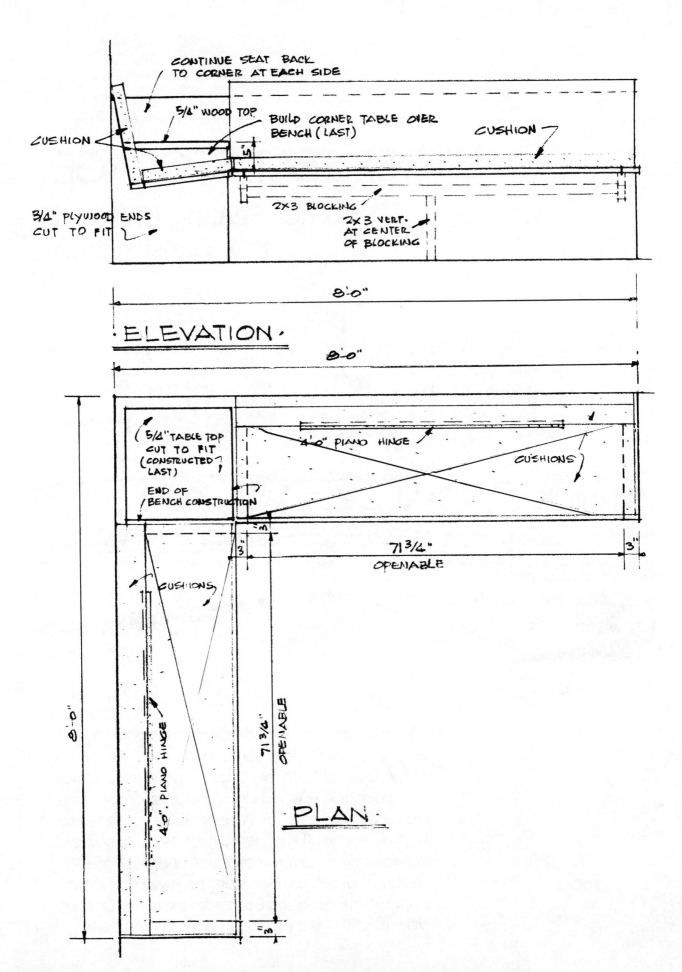

CONTINUE SEAT BACK
TO CORNER AT EACH SIDE

5/4" WOOD TOP

BUILD CORNER TABLE OVER
BENCH (LAST)

CUSHION

CUSHION

CUSHION

3/4" PLYWOOD ENDS
CUT TO FIT

2X3 BLOCKING

2X3 VERT.
AT CENTER
OF BLOCKING

5"

8'-0"

· ELEVATION ·

8'-0"

(5/4" TABLE TOP
CUT TO FIT
(CONSTRUCTED
LAST)

END OF
BENCH CONSTRUCTION

4'-0" PIANO HINGE

CUSHIONS

71 3/4"
OPENABLE

3"

3"

CUSHIONS

4'-0" PIANO HINGE

8'-0"

71 3/4"
OPENABLE

3"

PLAN

CORNER SEAT
WITH STORAGE UNDER

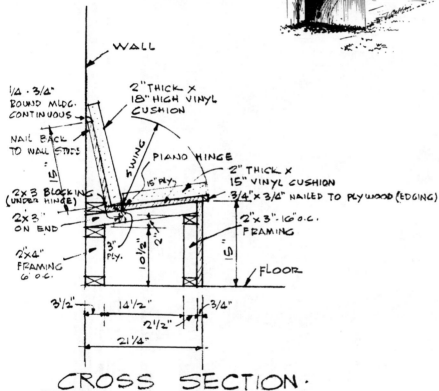

WALL

1/4 · 3/4" ROUND MLDG. CONTINUOUS

2" THICK X 18" HIGH VINYL CUSHION

NAIL BACK TO WALL STUDS

PIANO HINGE

SWING

15" PLY.

2" THICK X 15" VINYL CUSHION

3/4" X 3/4" NAILED TO PLYWOOD (EDGING)

2 X 3 BLOCKING (UNDER HINGE)

2 X 3 ON END

2"X 3"- 16" O.C. FRAMING

3" PLY.

10 1/2"

2"

5"

2"X4" FRAMING 6' O.C.

FLOOR

3 1/2"   14 1/2"   3/4"

2 1/2"

21 1/4"

CROSS SECTION.

MATERIAL LIST

8	2x4's @ 8'-0"
10	2x3's @ 8'-0"
6	3/4" x 15" PLYWOOD (BIRCH FINISH)
2	3/4" x 3" " (" ")
1	3/4" x 4' x 4" PLYWOOD (BIRCH) CUT FOR ENDS
1	5/4" x 20" x 20" TABLE TOP (CUT TO FIT)
2	3/4" x 3/4" SEAT EDGING
2	3/4" - 1/4" ROUND SEAT TOP
2	4'-0" PIANO HINGES
2	77"N x 2"THICK x 18"HIGH VINYL CUSHIONS
2	" x " x 15" SEAT " "

11.

LIVING WALL WITH SEATING
The cushioned bench helps out at a buffet party

A handyman can save money by building furniture. The unit pictured, for example, provides seating plus storage. The seating is in the form of a cushioned bench that tops four roomy bins with drop-down doors that store toys, games, you name it. Shelves at either side store a library of books and show off bric-a-brac. Unit is 9 feet, 2 inches wide; seat, 15½ inches deep; shelves 9½ inches deep.

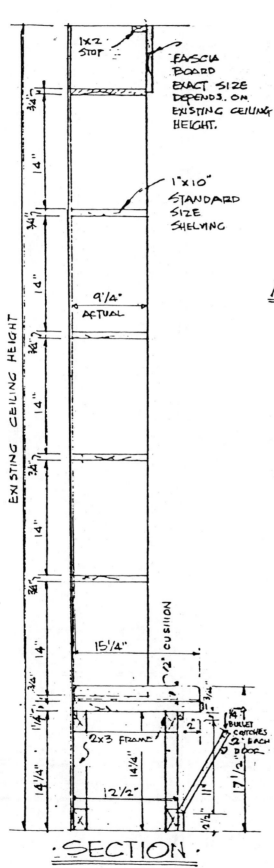

SECTION

MATERIAL LIST

54 LIN. FT.	1"x10"	SHELVING
9'-2"	1"xHT.	FASCIA BOARD
9'-0½"	1¼"x15¼"	BENCH TOP
9'	1"x12"	DOORS (CUT)
9'	1"x 3"	BOTTOM FRONT (CUT)
13'	¾"x ¾"	FRONT FRAME (CUT)
2'-6"	¾"x6"	SIDES SEAT (CUT)
9'	1"x2"	STOP (TOP)
51 LIN. FT.	2x3"	SEAT FRAME
1		4x8 PRE-FINISHED PANEL (BACKING, CUT)
2 PAIR		CONCEALED TYPE HINGES
4	KNOBS	DOORS
8		½"⌀ BULLET CATCHES 8 ASSEMBLY

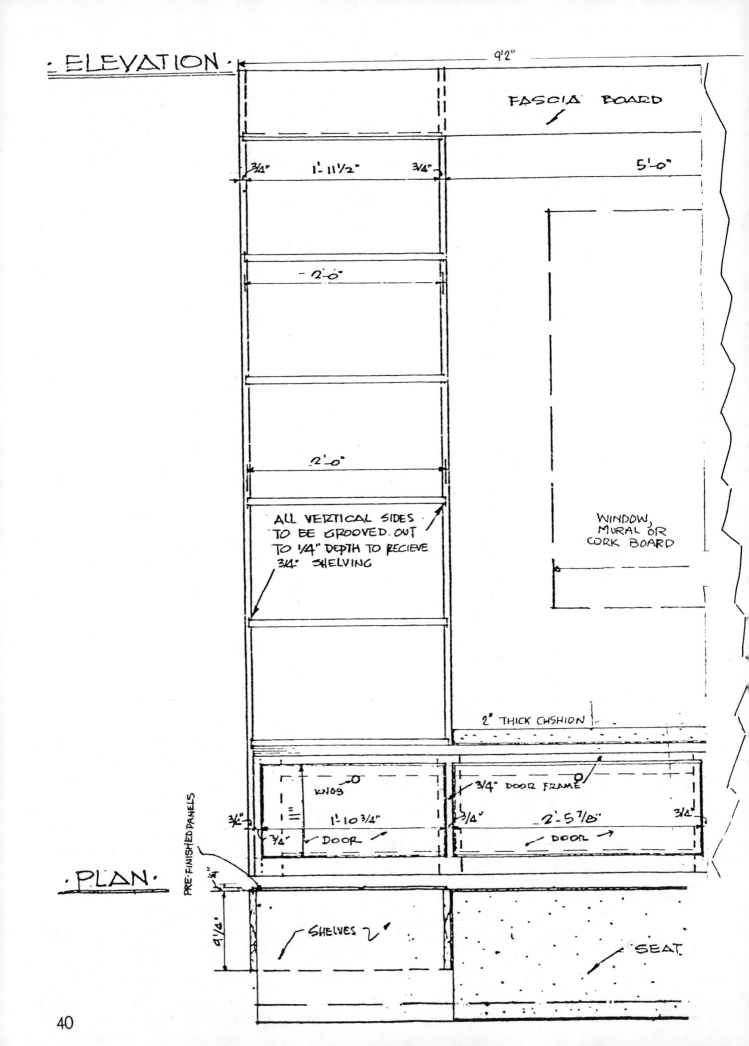

· ELEVATION ·

9'2"

FASCIA BOARD

3/4"   1'-11½"   3/4"   5'-0"

- 2'-0"

2'-0"

ALL VERTICAL SIDES
TO BE GROOVED. OUT
TO ¼" DEPTH TO RECIEVE
¾" SHELVING

WINDOW,
MURAL OR
CORK BOARD

2" THICK CUSHION

KNOB   ⊙   ¾" DOOR FRAME   ⊙

PRE-FINISHED PANELS

3/4"   1'-10¾"   3/4"   2'-5⅞"   3/4"

3/4"   DOOR   DOOR

· PLAN ·

¼"

9¼"

SHELVES 2'   SEAT

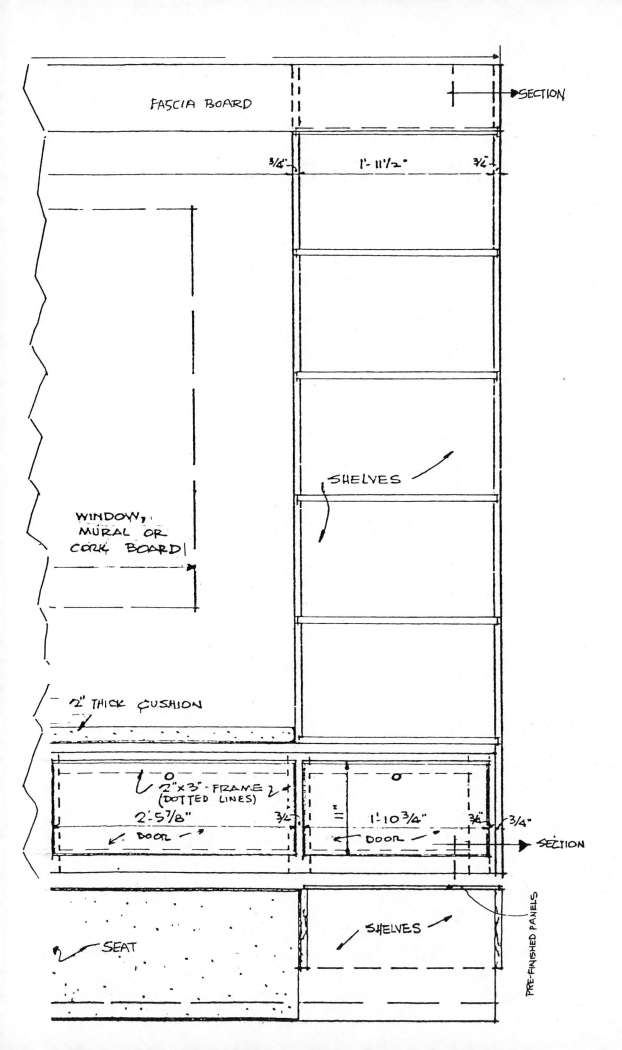

FASCIA BOARD

3/8"   1'-11 1/2"   3/4"

SECTION

SHELVES

WINDOW,
MURAL OR
CORK BOARD

2" THICK CUSHION

2"x3"-FRAME
(DOTTED LINES)
2'-5 7/8"

3/4"

DOOR

1'-10 3/4"   3/4"   3/4"

DOOR

SECTION

SEAT

SHELVES

PRE-FINISHED PANELS

41

DESK & STOWAWAY UNITS

12.

BIG DESK SPACE
Provides handy desk plus stowaway space

If you need a desk plus stowaway space, this design could solve all your problems. Ideal for a child's or family room, it's simple to build. A standard size hollow core door is used for desk top. Open shelves hold books, TV, whatever. Cabinets provide more storage space, while drawers file important papers. Storage wall-desk is 6 feet 9½ inches wide; 11¼ inches deep (desk depth, 1 foot 8 inches); 7 feet high.

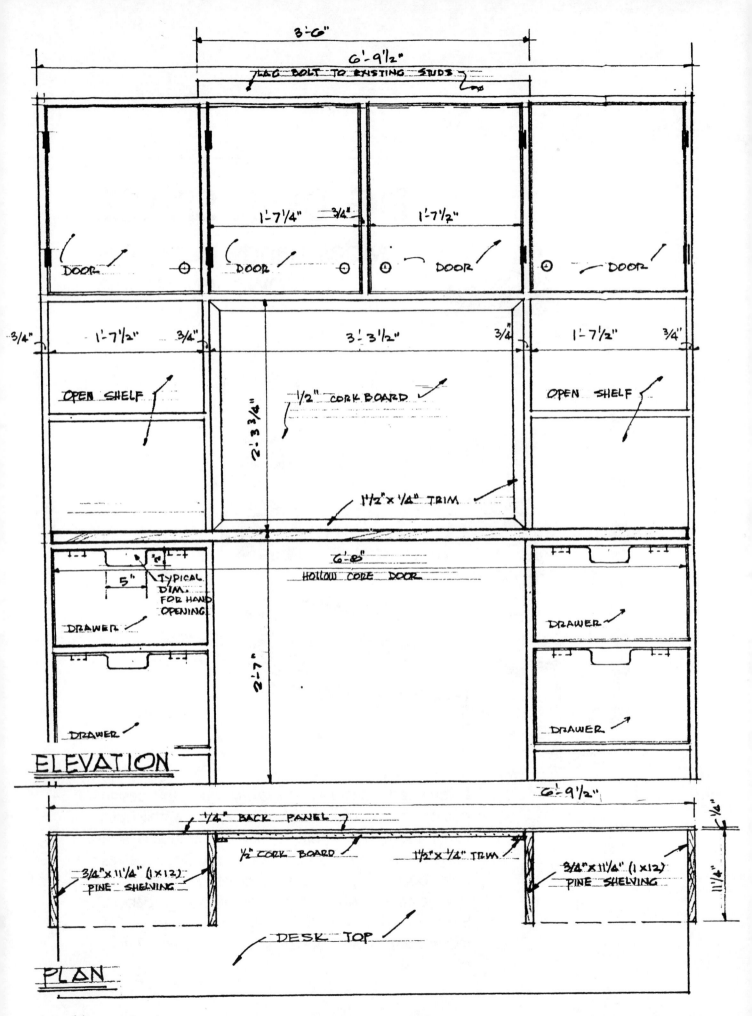

ELEVATION

PLAN

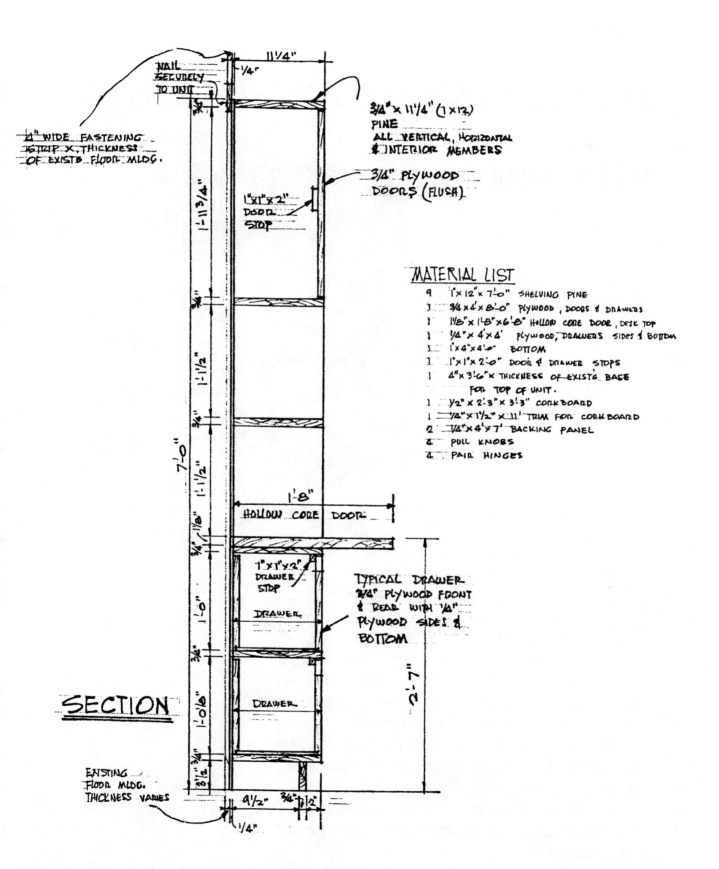

NAIL SECURELY TO UNIT

4" WIDE FASTENING STRIP X THICKNESS OF EXISTG FLOOR MLDG.

11¼"

¼"

3/4" x 11¼" (1 x 12) PINE
ALL VERTICAL, HORIZONTAL & INTERIOR MEMBERS

3/4" PLYWOOD DOORS (FLUSH)

1"x1"x2" DOOR STOP

1'-11¾"

3/4"

1'-1½"

3/4"

7'-0"

1'-1½"

1⅛"

3/4"

1'-8"

HOLLOW CORE DOOR

MATERIAL LIST

9	1"x 12"x 7'-0"	SHELVING PINE
1	3/4 x 4'x 8'-0"	PLYWOOD, DOORS & DRAWERS
1	1⅜"x 1'-8"x 6'-8"	HOLLOW CORE DOOR, DESK TOP
1	¼"x 4'x 4'	PLYWOOD, DRAWERS SIDES & BOTTOM
1	1"x 4"x 4'-0"	BOTTOM
1	1"x1"x 2'-0"	DOOR & DRAWER STOPS
1	4"x 3'-6"x THICKNESS OF EXISTG	BASE
		FOR TOP OF UNIT.
1	½"x 2'-3"x 3'-3"	CORKBOARD
1	¼"x 1½"x 11'	TRIM FOR CORKBOARD
2	¼"x 4'x 7'	BACKING PANEL
4	PULL KNOBS	
4	PAIR HINGES	

1"x1"x2" DRAWER STOP

DRAWER

TYPICAL DRAWER 3/4" PLYWOOD FRONT & REAR WITH ¼" PLYWOOD SIDES & BOTTOM

2'-7"

1'-0"

3/4"

1'-0⅛"

DRAWER

3/4"

3½"

EXISTING FLOOR MLDG. THICKNESS VARIES

9½"   3/4" ½"

¼"

SECTION

13.

HOME MANAGEMENT CENTER

The entire family will find it useful

If the family room is the gathering spot for your clan, this easy-to-build desk could be a handy addition. It is designed with generous storage space for family records and bills and for home office supplies. Mom can use it when she plans menus or writes out store lists. The children will utilize it for homework. Dad can spread out tax papers or the family bookkeeping when the first of the month rolls around.

The desk is planned with shelves, mail bins and drawers. There is a corkboard panel at back that's handy for pinning up recipes or memos.

The desk, 4 feet wide by 5 feet, 6 inches high by 9¾ inches deep, could also be useful in a dinette or a child's bedroom.

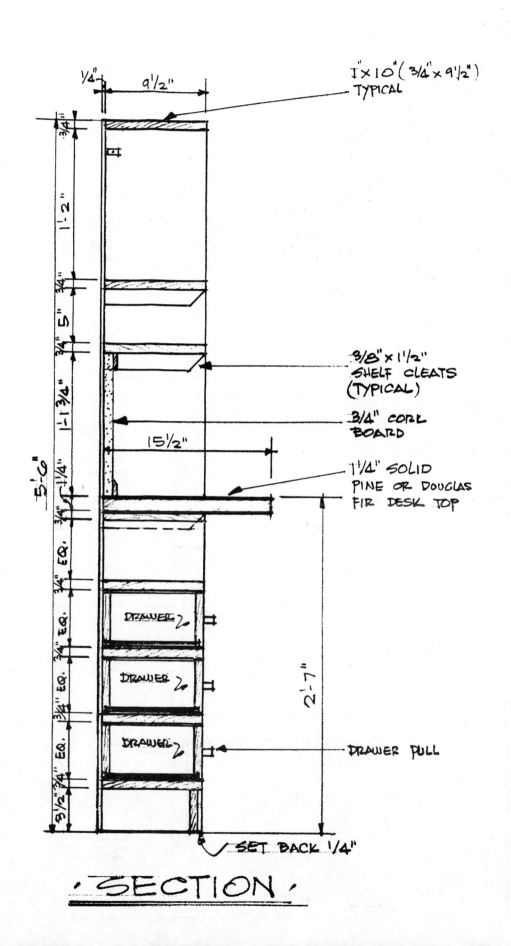

1"×10" (3/4" × 9 1/2")
TYPICAL

1/4"

9 1/2"

3/4"

1'-2"

3/4"

5"

3/4"

3/8" × 1 1/2"
SHELF CLEATS
(TYPICAL)

1'-3 3/4"

3/4" CORE
BOARD

15 1/2"

1 1/4"

1 1/4" SOLID
PINE OR DOUGLAS
FIR DESK TOP

3/4"

3/4" EQ.

5'-6"

3/4" EQ.

2'-7"

DRAWER

3/4" EQ.

DRAWER

3/4" EQ.

DRAWER

DRAWER PULL

3/4"

3 1/2"

SET BACK 1/4"

· SECTION ·

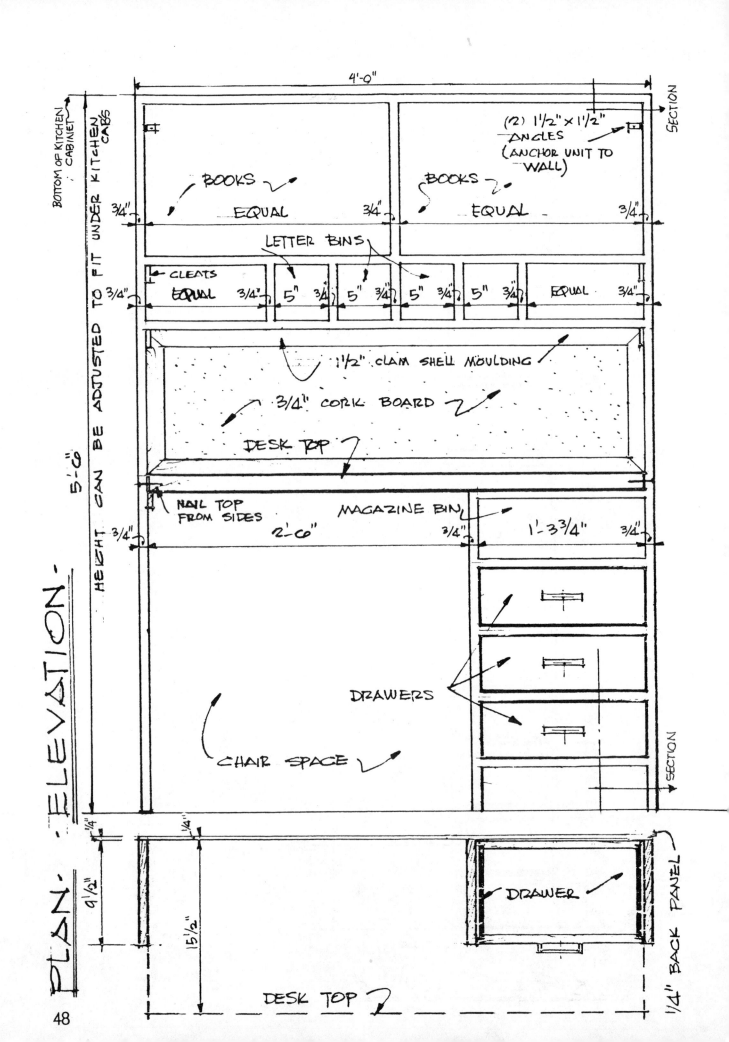

BOTTOM OF KITCHEN CABINET

4'-0"

(2) 1½" x 1½" ANGLES (ANCHOR UNIT TO WALL)

SECTION

BOOKS

BOOKS

EQUAL

EQUAL

¾"

¾"

¾"

LETTER BINS

CLEATS

EQUAL

¾"

5"

¾"

5"

¾"

5"

¾"

5"

¾"

EQUAL

¾"

¾"

1½" CLAM SHELL MOULDING

¾" CORK BOARD

DESK TOP

HEIGHT CAN BE ADJUSTED TO FIT UNDER KITCHEN CABS

5'-0"

NAIL TOP FROM SIDES

MAGAZINE BIN

¾"

2'-6"

¾"

1'-3¾"

¾"

DRAWERS

CHAIR SPACE

SECTION

ELEVATION

PLAN

¼"

¼"

9½"

15½"

DRAWER

¼" BACK PANEL

DESK TOP

48

MATERIAL LIST

1 SHEET 4'-0" X 7'-0" X 1/4" BACK PANEL & DRAWERS
39 LIN.FT.-1X10 (3/4"X 9 1/2) SHELVING & SIDES
8 LIN.FT- "   "   DRAWERS (FRONT & BACK
5 LIN.FT.-3/8" X 1 1/2" SHELF CLEATS
       1'-1" X 3'-10" X 3/4" CORK BOARD
17 LIN.FT.-1 1/2" CLAM SHELL MOULDING
  1 - 3/4" X 3 1/2" X 1'- 4"
  3 - DRAWER PULLS
  1 - 1 1/4" X 15 1/2" X 4'-0" SOLID PINE OR FIR DESK TOP
  2 - 1 1/2" X 1 1/2" ANGLES

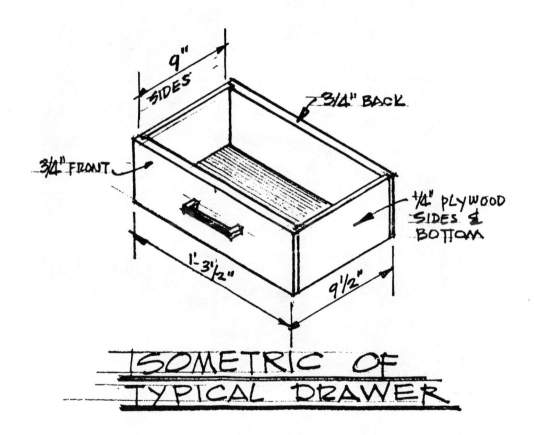

9"
SIDES

3/4" BACK

3/4" FRONT

1/4" PLYWOOD
SIDES &
BOTTOM

1'-3 1/2"

9 1/2"

ISOMETRIC OF TYPICAL DRAWER

14.

PAPERWORK HIDEAWAY
A compact work center

This home office unit is designed to keep 9 to 5 office hours. You can close up shop by closing the louvered doors. Desk setup includes drawers, bins and shelves to store books, papers, and other aids. Built-in light illuminates desk top. Office is 5 feet, 4¼ inches wide; 15¾ inches deep; height can be adapted to 7 or 8 feet.

· MATERIAL LIST ·

35	LIN. FT.	3/4" × 15 3/4" PLYWOOD CUT FROM 4×8 SHEETS
6	LIN. FT.	3/4" × 11 1/2" TOP FRONT
17	LIN. FT.	3/4" × 9 1/4" SHELVES
12	LIN. FT.	3/4" × 7 3/4" FRONT & REAR OF BOTTOM DRAWERS
6	LIN. FT.	3/4" × 5 1/2" FRONT, BOOK SHELF
1		1/2" × 4'-2" × 1'-10" CORKBOARD
18	LIN. FT.	1/4" × 1 1/2" CLAMSHELL FOR CORKBOARD FRAME & SHELF EDGE

9	LIN. FT.	3/4" × 3 1/2" BOTTOM KICK & SMALL DRAWER, FRONT & BACK
1		16 1/2" × 5'-3" LAMINATED PLASTIC FOR DESK TOP
1	4' × 4'	3/8" PLYWOOD FOR DRAWERS SIDES & BOTTOM.
2	4' × 8"	1/4" PREFINISHED PLYWOOD FOR BACK
1	4'-0"	FLUORESCENT FIXTURE
5		PULL KNOBS

· SECTION B-B ·

· SECTION A-A ·

NOTE:
FRONT & REAR OF DRAWER TO BE 3/4", SIDES & BOTTOM 1/4" PLYWOOD

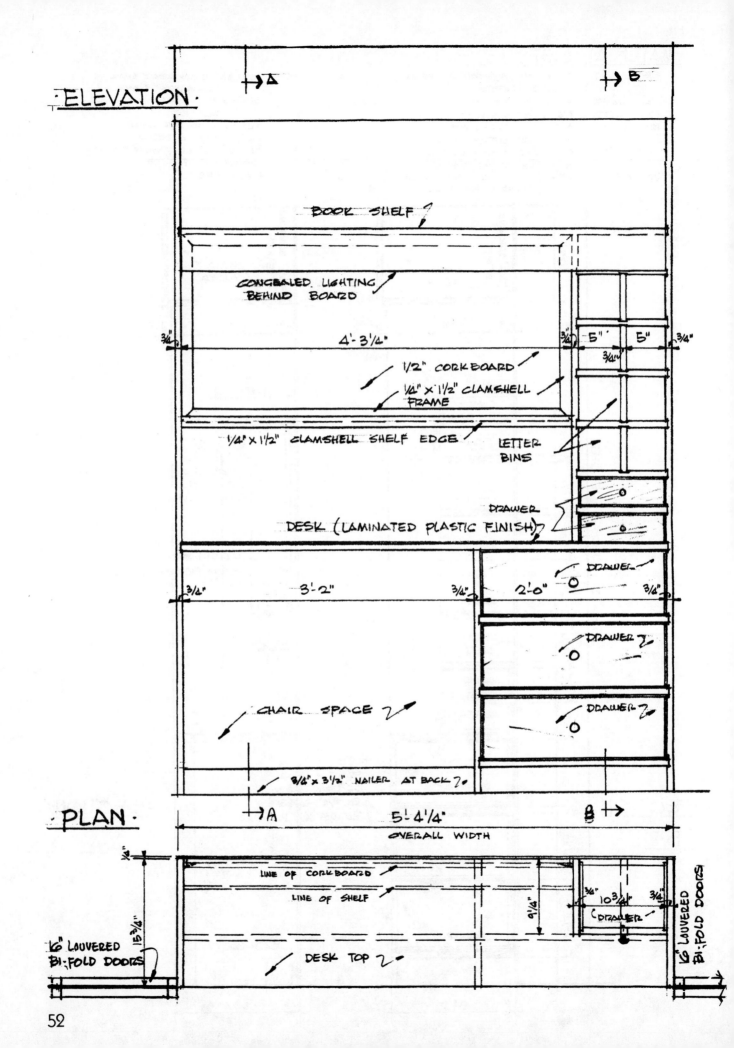

· ELEVATION ·

BOOK SHELF

CONCEALED LIGHTING BEHIND BOARD

4'-3¼"   ¾"   5"   5"   ¾"
¾"   ¾"

½" CORKBOARD

¼" × 1½" CLAMSHELL FRAME

¼" × 1½" CLAMSHELL SHELF EDGE

LETTER BINS

DRAWER

DESK (LAMINATED PLASTIC FINISH)

¾"   3'-2"   ¾"   2'-0"   DRAWER   ¾"

DRAWER

DRAWER

CHAIR SPACE

3/4" × 3½" NAILER AT BACK

· PLAN ·   5'-4¼"
                OVERALL WIDTH

A   B

¼"

LINE OF CORKBOARD

LINE OF SHELF

9¼"

¾" 10¾" ¾"

DRAWER

15¾"

16" LOUVERED BI-FOLD DOORS

DESK TOP

16" LOUVERED BI-FOLD DOORS

52

OPEN BOOKCASE WALL

Bookcase with desk and area for stereo

Need a catchall for odds and ends? This bookcase unit could be it. At one side, there's a desk and, above it, small drawers for office supplies. At the other side, sliding doors conceal a stereo.

The bookcase is made up of two 4-foot units. You can build one or both, as you prefer. As pictured, it is 9 feet, 6 inches wide, including end panels, by 7 feet, 9½ inches high by 11¼ inches deep.

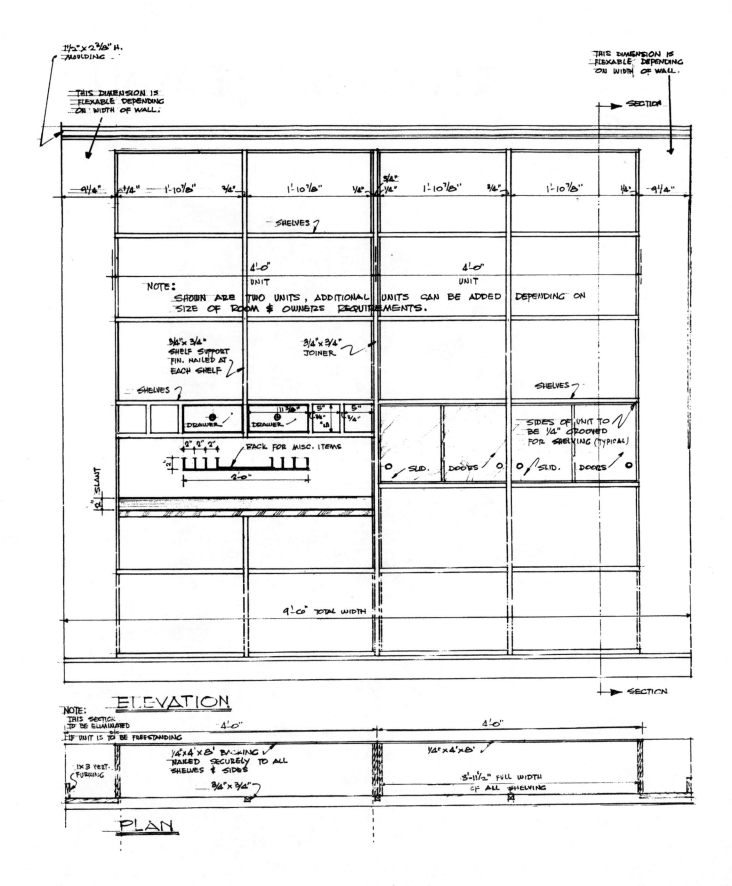

1½" x 2⅜" H.
MOULDING

THIS DIMENSION IS
FLEXABLE DEPENDING
ON WIDTH OF WALL.

THIS DIMENSION IS
FLEXABLE DEPENDING
ON WIDTH OF WALL.

SECTION

9¼"   2¼"   1'-10⅞"   ¾"   1'-10⅞"   ¼"   ¾"   1'-10⅞"   ¾"   1'-10⅞"   ¼"   9¼"

SHELVES

4'-0"
UNIT

4'-0"
UNIT

NOTE:
SHOWN ARE TWO UNITS, ADDITIONAL UNITS CAN BE ADDED DEPENDING ON
SIZE OF ROOM & OWNERS REQUIREMENTS.

¾"x ¾"
SHELF SUPPORT
FIN. NAILED AT
EACH SHELF

¾"x ¾"
JOINER

SHELVES

SHELVES

DRAWER   DRAWER   1 1⅜"   5"   5"
¾"   ¾"

SIDES OF UNIT TO
BE ¼" GROOVED
FOR SHELVING (TYPICAL)

2"   2"   2"   RACK FOR MISC. ITEMS

2"

2"   2'-0"

2" SLANT

O   SLID.   DOORS   O   O   SLID.   DOORS   O

9'-0" TOTAL WIDTH

SECTION

ELEVATION

NOTE:
THIS SECTION
TO BE ELIMINATED
IF UNIT IS TO BE FREESTANDING

4'-0"

4'-0"

1X3 VERT.
FURRING

¼"x4'x8' BACKING
NAILED SECURELY TO ALL
SHELVES & SIDES

¼"x4'x8'

¾"x ¾"

3'-11½" FULL WIDTH
OF ALL SHELVING

PLAN

54

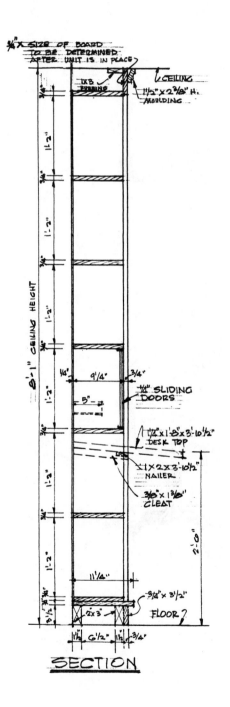

¾" X SIZE OF BOARD
TO BE DETERMINED
AFTER UNIT IS IN PLACE

1X3 FURRING

CEILING

1½" x 2⅜" H.
MOULDING

2'-1"

8'-1" CEILING HEIGHT

¾"   1'-2"

9¼"   ¾"

¼" SLIDING
DOORS

5"

1¼" x 1'-8" x 3'-10½"
DESK TOP

1 X 2 X 3'-10½"
NAILER

3/8" x 1 3/8"
CLEAT

2'-0"

11¼"

¾" x 3½"

2x3

FLOOR

1½"   6½"   1½"   ¾"

SECTION

MATERIAL LIST

¾" X 9¼" X 90 LIN. FT. SHELVING
¾" X ¾" X 24 LIN FT. VERT. SUPPORTS
(2)   ½" X 9¼" X 8' VERTICAL ENDS
(1)   ¾" X VARIABLE DEPTH TOP PIECE
(1)   1½" X 2⅜" X WIDTH OF UNIT (TOP MLDG)
(1)   1¼" X 1'-8" X 3'-10½" DESK TOP
(1)   1X2 X 3'-10½" NAILER
(1)   3/8" X 1 3/8" X 2'-0" CLEAT (UNDER DESK)
   1 3/16" X ½" X 4'-0" TOP PRE-GROOVED TRACK
   1 1/16" X 3/8" X 4'-0" BOTTOM "   "   "
   ¼" X 1'-1½" X 6'-0" PLYWOOD FOR SLID. DOORS
                                    & DRAWERS
   ¼" X 5" X 6' PLYWOOD FOR DRAWER,
             & MISC. RACK
(1)   ¾" X 11¼" X 9'-6" BOTTOM SHELF
(1)   ¾" X 3½" X 9'-6" BOTTOM TOE STRIP
(2)   2X3 X 9'-6" BOTTOM FRAMING
(1)   1X3 X 9'-6" TOP FURRING
(2)   ¼" X 4'-0" X 8'-0" BACKING PANEL

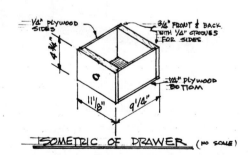

¼" PLYWOOD
SIDES

¾" FRONT & BACK
WITH ¼" GROOVES
FOR SIDES

4¾"

¼" PLYWOOD
BOTTOM

11⅛"   9¼"

ISOMETRIC OF DRAWER (NO SCALE)

16.

CABINET STORAGE WITH DESK

It has a place for everything

Here's a plan to solve all your where-to-put-it problems. A roomy design, it provides stowaway shelves for books plus overhead and lower cabinets that can stash a variety of odds and ends from bulky serving pieces and games to out-of-season items.

The big plus is a drop-down desk. As shown, it's 8 feet wide but it can be built as a 4-foot or 12-foot unit; 8 feet high; lower cabinets, 13¼ inches deep; shelves, 9¼ inches deep.

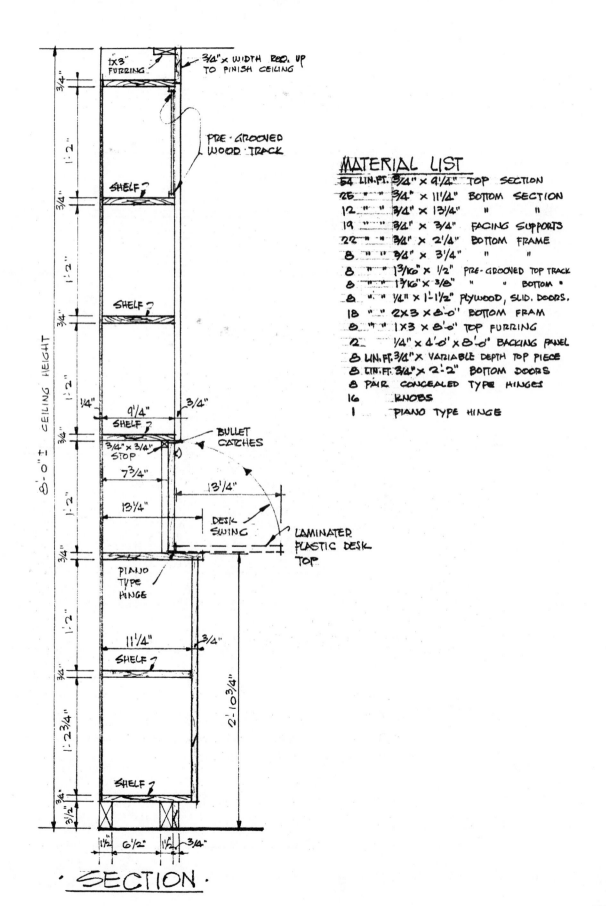

MATERIAL LIST

54 LIN.FT. 3/4" x 9 1/4" TOP SECTION
25 " " 3/4" x 11 1/4" BOTTOM SECTION
12 " " 3/4" x 13 1/4" " "
19 " " 3/4" x 3/4" FACING SUPPORTS
22 " " 3/4" x 2 1/4" BOTTOM FRAME
8 " " 3/4" x 3/4" " "
8 " " 13/16" x 1/2" PRE-GROOVED TOP TRACK
8 " " 13/16" x 3/8" " BOTTOM "
2 " " 1/4" x 1-1 1/2" PLYWOOD, SLID. DOORS.
18 " " 2 x 3 x 8'-0' BOTTOM FRAM
8 " " 1 x 3 x 8'-0' TOP FURRING
2 1/4" x 4'-0' x 8'-0' BACKING PANEL
8 LIN. FT. 3/4" x VARIABLE DEPTH TOP PIECE
8 LIN. FT. 3/4" x 2'-2' BOTTOM DOORS
8 PAIR CONCEALED TYPE HINGES
16 KNOBS
1 PIANO TYPE HINGE

1 x 3" FURRING
3/4" x WIDTH REQ. UP TO FINISH CEILING
PRE-GROOVED WOOD TRACK
SHELF
SHELF
SHELF
BULLET CATCHES
3/4" x 3/4" STOP
DESK SWING
LAMINATED PLASTIC DESK TOP
PIANO TYPE HINGE
SHELF
SHELF

3/4"
1'-2"
3/4"
1'-2"
3/4"
1'-2"
1/4"
3/4"
9 1/4"
3/4"
7 3/4"
13 1/4"
13 1/4"
3/4"
1'-2"
11 1/4"
3/4"
3/4"
1'-2 3/4"
3/4"
3/2"
2'-10 3/4"

± 8'-0" CEILING HEIGHT

1 1/2" 6 1/2" 1 1/2" 3/4"

· SECTION ·

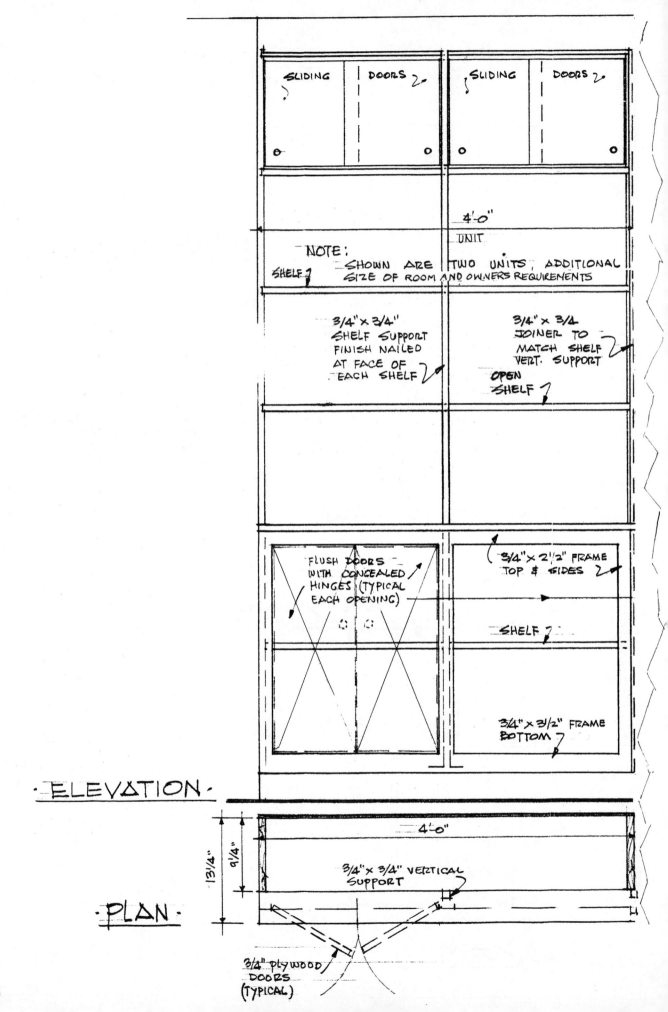

SLIDING | DOORS

SLIDING | DOORS

4'-0"
UNIT

NOTE:
SHOWN ARE TWO UNITS; ADDITIONAL
SIZE OF ROOM AND OWNERS REQUIREMENTS

SHELF

3/4" x 3/4"
SHELF SUPPORT
FINISH NAILED
AT FACE OF
EACH SHELF

3/4" x 3/4
JOINER TO
MATCH SHELF
VERT. SUPPORT

OPEN
SHELF

FLUSH DOORS
WITH CONCEALED
HINGES (TYPICAL
EACH OPENING)

3/4" x 2 1/2" FRAME
TOP & SIDES

SHELF

3/4" x 3 1/2" FRAME
BOTTOM

· ELEVATION ·

4'-0"

13 1/4"

9 1/4"

3/4" x 3/4" VERTICAL
SUPPORT

· PLAN ·

3/4" PLYWOOD
DOORS
(TYPICAL)

58

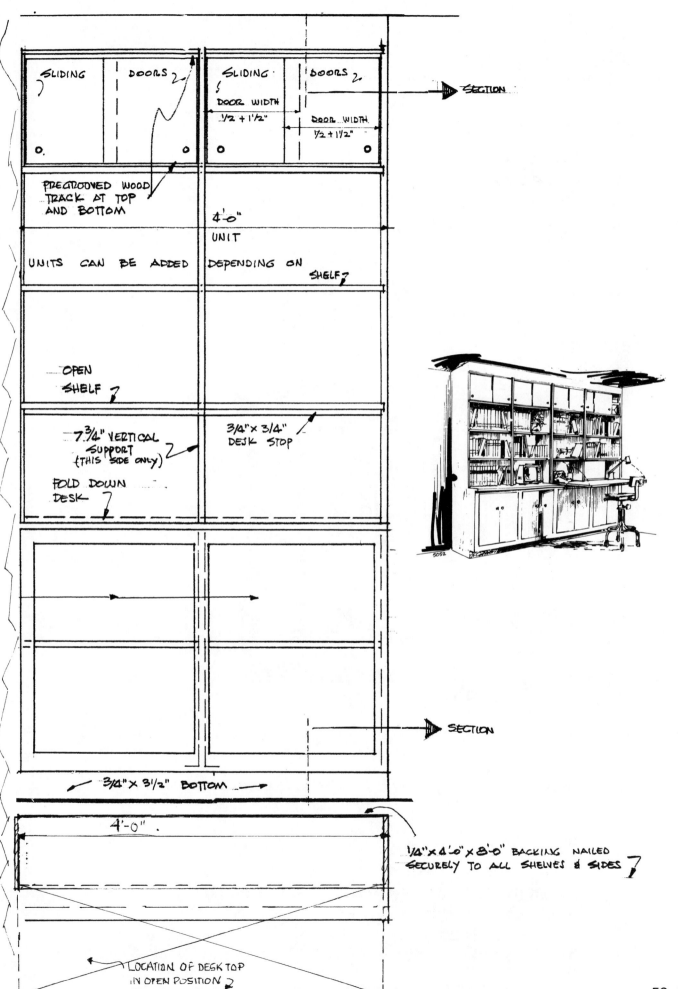

SLIDING   DOORS 2   SLIDING   DOORS 2

DOOR WIDTH   DOOR WIDTH
1/2 + 1'1/2"   1/2 + 1'1/2"

SECTION

PRECROOVED WOOD
TRACK AT TOP
AND BOTTOM

4'-0"

UNIT

UNITS CAN BE ADDED   DEPENDING ON

SHELF 7

OPEN
SHELF 7

3/4" x 3/4"
DESK STOP

7.3/4" VERTICAL
SUPPORT
(THIS SIDE ONLY)

FOLD DOWN
DESK 7

SECTION

3/4" x 3'1/2" BOTTOM

4'-0"

1/4" x 4'-0" x 8'-0" BACKING NAILED
SECURELY TO ALL SHELVES & SIDES 7

LOCATION OF DESK TOP
IN OPEN POSITION 2

17.
MODULAR CLOTHING STORAGE SYSTEM

To house your wardrobe

Need more storage space for clothing? Build this double 8-foot-wide closet—or build just one 4-foot unit. As shown, each unit has built-in drawers for lingerie, shirts, hosiery. Above drawers, there is hanging space for jackets, skirts, blouses. The other half of each closet has full-length hanging space for dresses and coats. Each unit is 2 feet, 1½ inches deep. Stain or paint to match decor.

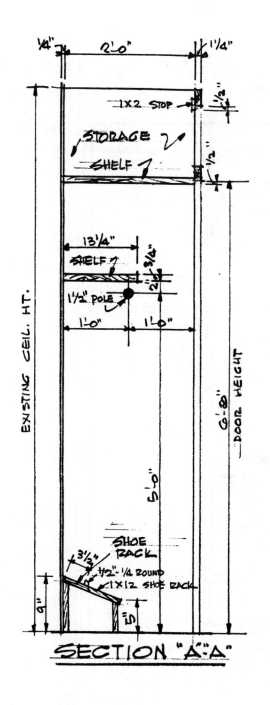

1/4" — 2'-0" — 1 1/4"

1X2 STOP — 1/2"

STORAGE
SHELF — 1/2"

13 1/4"
SHELF — 3/4"
1 1/2" POLE — 2"
1'-0" — 1'-0"

5'-0"

SHOE
RACK
3 1/2"
1/2"- 1/4 ROUND
1X12 SHOE RACK
9"
5"

EXISTING CEIL. HT.

6'-8" DOOR HEIGHT

SECTION "A"-"A"

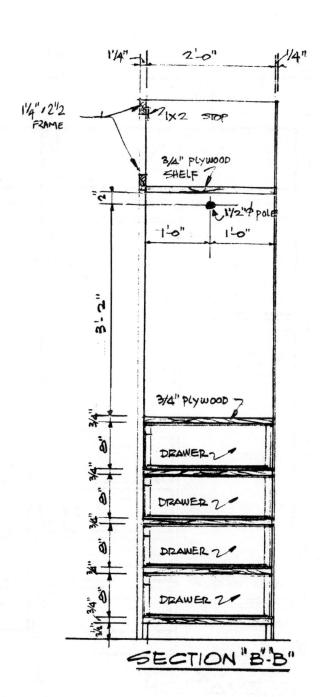

1 1/4" — 2'-0" — 1 1/4"

1 1/4" 2 1/2
FRAME
1X2 STOP

3/4" PLYWOOD
SHELF
2"
1 1/2"Ø POLE
1'-0" — 1'-0"

3'-2"

3/4" PLYWOOD
3/4" 8"
DRAWER
3/4" 8"
DRAWER
3/4" 8"
DRAWER
3/4" 8"
DRAWER
3/4"

SECTION "B"-"B"

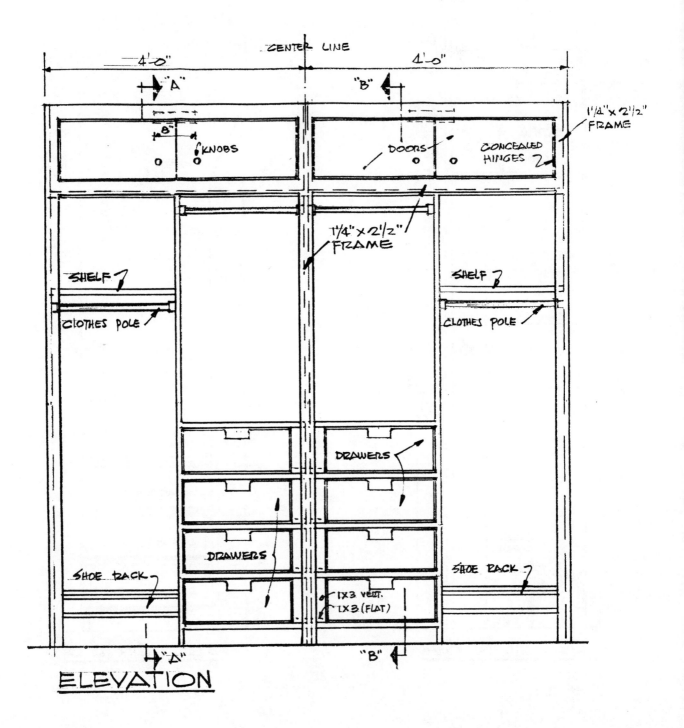

CENTER LINE

4'-0"   4'-0"

"A"   "B"

1¼"x 2½"
FRAME

KNOBS   DOORS   CONCEALED HINGES

1¼"x 2½"
FRAME

SHELF   SHELF

CLOTHES POLE   CLOTHES POLE

DRAWERS

DRAWERS

SHOE RACK   SHOE RACK

1X3 VERT.
1X3 (FLAT)

"A"   "B"

ELEVATION

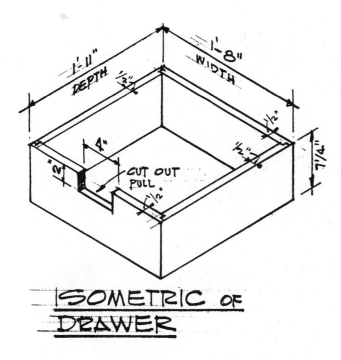

ISOMETRIC OF DRAWER

DEPTH 1'-11"
WIDTH 1'-8"
7 1/4"
CUT OUT PULL
4"

MATERIAL LIST

7	3/4" x 2'-0" x 8' PLYWOOD
1	3/4" x 11 1/4" x 4' ⎫ SHOE RACK
1	3/4" x 6" x 4' ⎬
1	3/4" x 9 1/2" x 4' ⎭
1	3/4" x 13 1/4" x 4' CLOSET SHELF
1	1 1/2"⌀ x 8' CLOTHES POLE
32 FT.	1/2" x 7 1/4" DRAWER SIDES, FRONT, REAR
2	1/4" x 8' PLYWOOD FOR DRAWER BOTTOMS
1	1" x 2" x 10" TOP DOOR STOPS
1	3/4" x 1'-0" x 8' PLYWOOD DOORS, TOP (CUT TO FIT)
5	1 1/4" x 2 1/2" x 8' FRONT FRAME
4	1 1/4" x 15" x 6'-8" LOUVERED CLOSET DOORS (CUT TO FIT)
1	1/2" x 4' QUARTER ROUND FOR SHOE RACK
10	PAIR CONCEALED HINGES (2 PAIR FOR EACH TOP DOOR) (3 " " " CLOSET DOOR)
8	PULL KNOBS
22 FT	1X3 DRAWER SIDE & TRACK
2	4' X 8' PRE-FINISHED PLYWOOD BACKING

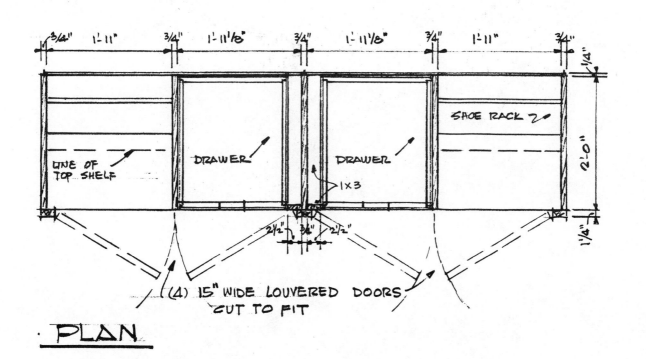

3/4" 1'-11" 3/4" 1'-11 1/8" 3/4" 1'-11 1/8" 3/4" 1'-11" 3/4"

1/4"
2'-0"
1/4"

LINE OF TOP SHELF
DRAWER
DRAWER
1X3
SHOE RACK
2 1/2" 3/4" 2 1/2"

(4) 15" WIDE LOUVERED DOORS CUT TO FIT

PLAN

HOSPITALITY

18

HIDEAWAY BAR
It disappears when not in use

This hideaway bar does a disappearing act when not in use. The awning folds down, the bar up; the entire unit is concealed behind doors. Although shown as a built-in, the bar can be built free-standing. Cabinets on either side plus base cabinets provide generous storage space·for bottles, glasses and serving pieces. Unit is 8 feet wide; 16⅛ inches deep. Build it room height.

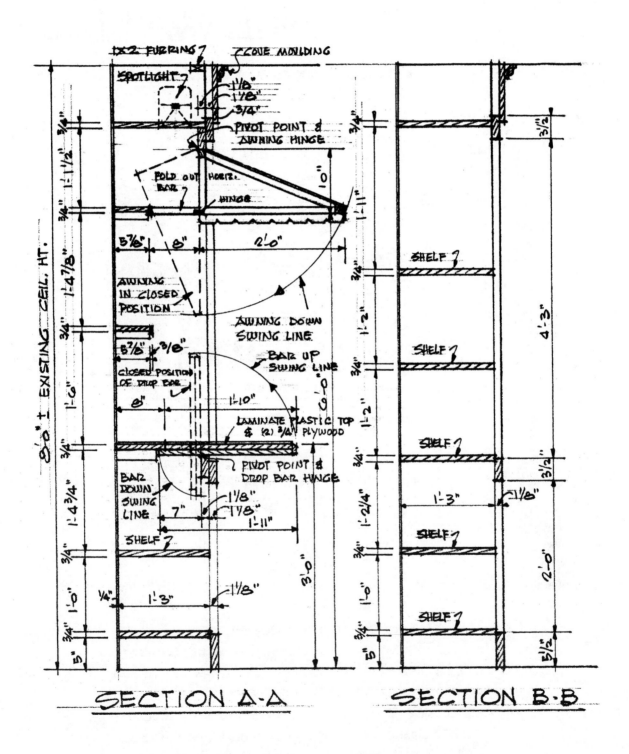

SECTION A·A SECTION B·B

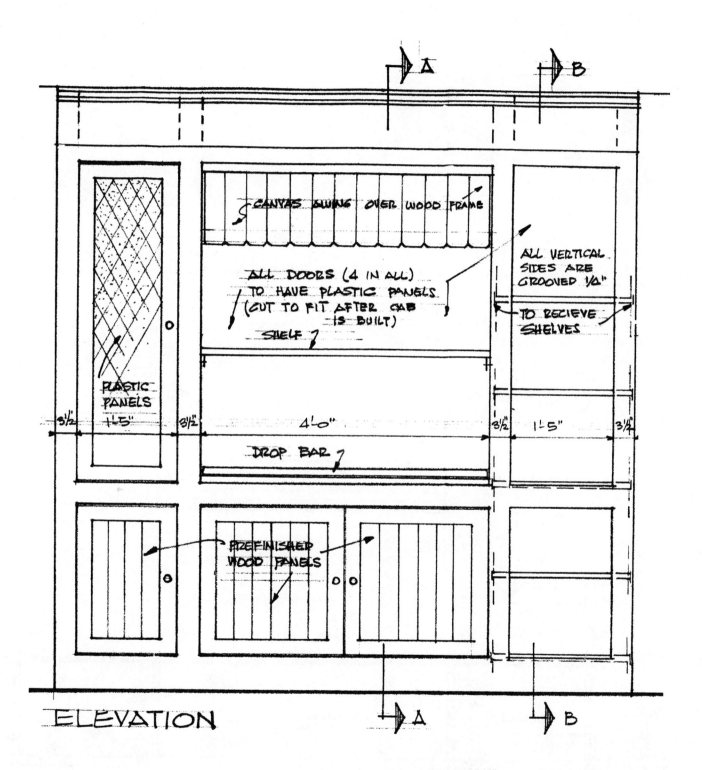

CANVAS SWING OVER WOOD FRAME

ALL DOORS (4 IN ALL) TO HAVE PLASTIC PANELS (CUT TO FIT AFTER CAB IS BUILT)

SHELF

PLASTIC PANELS

ALL VERTICAL SIDES ARE GROOVED 1/8" TO RECIEVE SHELVES

3½" | 1'-5" | 3½" | 4'-0" | 3½" | 1'-5" | 3½"

DROP BAR

PREFINISHED WOOD PANELS

ELEVATION

A   B

67

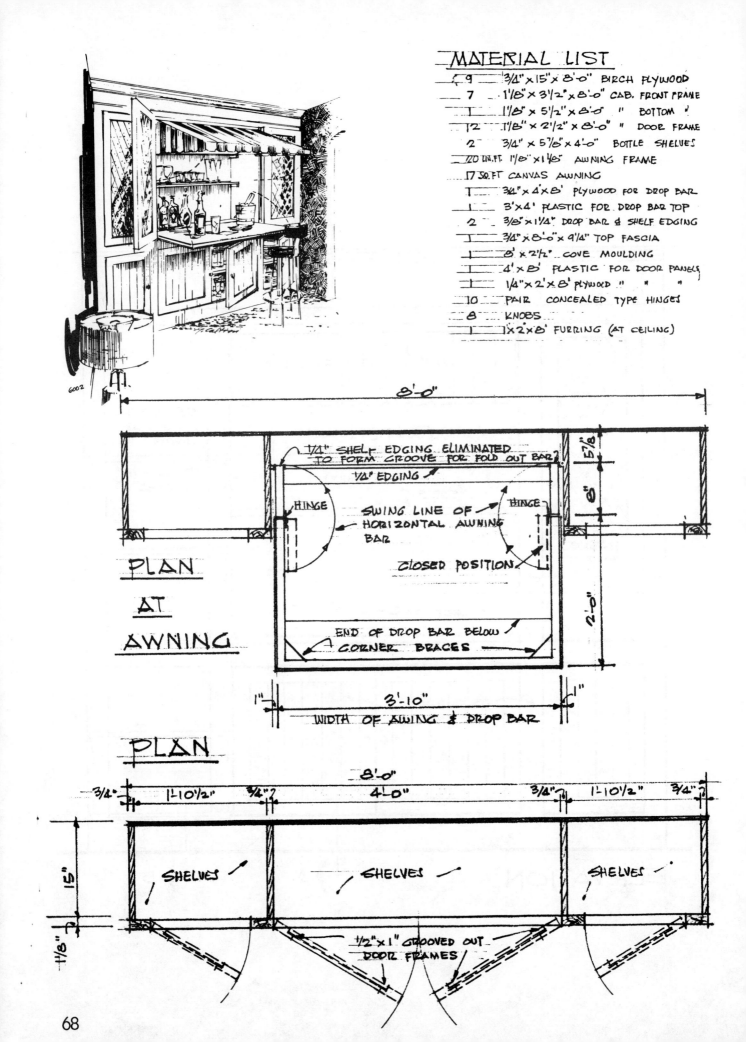

MATERIAL LIST

9	3/4" x 15" x 8'-0"	BIRCH PLYWOOD
7	1 1/8" x 3 1/2" x 8'-0"	CAB. FRONT FRAME
1	1 1/8" x 5 1/2" x 8'-0"	" BOTTOM
12	1 1/8" x 2 1/2" x 8'-0"	" DOOR FRAME
2	3/4" x 5 7/8" x 4'-0"	BOTTLE SHELVES
20 LIN. FT.	1 1/8" x 1 1/4"	AWNING FRAME
17 SQ. FT	CANVAS AWNING	
1	3/4" x 4' x 8'	PLYWOOD FOR DROP BAR
1	3' x 4'	PLASTIC FOR DROP BAR TOP
2	3/8" x 1 1/4"	DROP BAR & SHELF EDGING
1	3/4" x 8'-0" x 9 1/4"	TOP FASCIA
1	8' x 2 1/2"	COVE MOULDING
1	4' x 8'	PLASTIC FOR DOOR PANELS
1	1/4" x 2' x 8'	PLYWOOD " " "
10	PAIR	CONCEALED TYPE HINGES
8	KNOBS	
1	1 x 2 x 8'	FURRING (AT CEILING)

6002

8'-0"

5/8"

6"

1/4" SHELF EDGING ELIMINATED
TO FORM GROOVE FOR FOLD OUT BAR

1/4" EDGING

HINGE

SWING LINE OF
HORIZONTAL AWNING
BAR

HINGE

CLOSED POSITION

PLAN

AT

AWNING

END OF DROP BAR BELOW

CORNER BRACES

2'-0"

1" 3'-10" 1"

WIDTH OF AWING & DROP BAR

PLAN

8'-0"

3/4" 1'-10 1/2" 3/4" 4'-0" 3/4" 1'-10 1/2" 3/4"

15"

SHELVES   SHELVES   SHELVES

1/8"

1/2" x 1" GROOVED OUT
DOOR FRAMES

19.

DISHES & GLASSES HUTCH

Easy-to-build bar and storage cabinet is great when you entertain

If your family has entertaining ways, this build-it-yourself bar could be a decorative and useful addition to living room, den or play room. The drop leaf (shown open) provides a work counter for mixing drinks. Sliding doors front compartments for bottles, glasses and other supplies. Compact in size, the unit is 4 feet wide by 6 feet, 8 inches high by 8¾ inches deep.

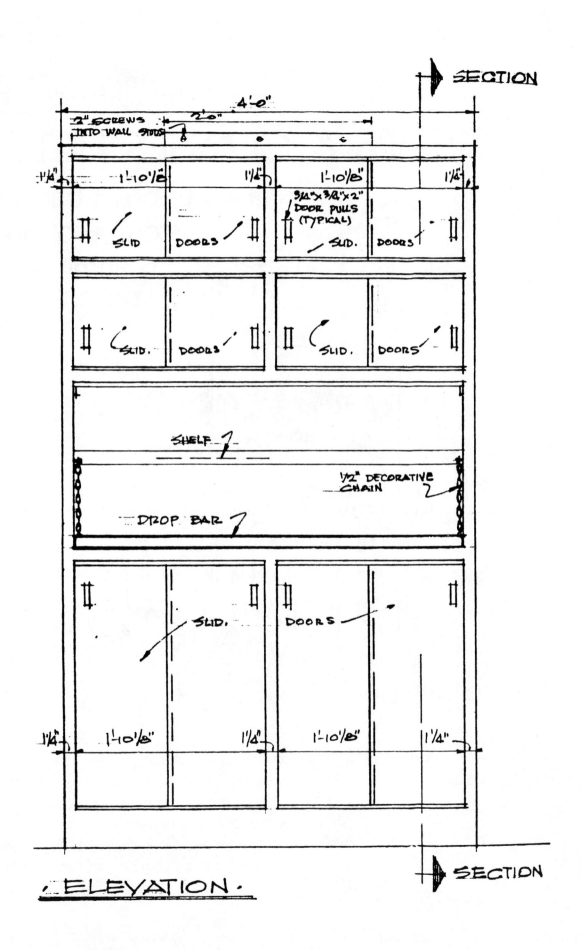

SECTION

2" SCREWS
INTO WALL STUDS

4'-0"

2'-0"

1'-4" 1'-10 1/8" 1 1/4" 1'-10 1/8" 1 1/4"

3/4"x 3/4"x 2"
DOOR PULLS
(TYPICAL)

SLID. DOORS SLID. DOORS

SLID. DOORS SLID. DOORS

SHELF

1/2" DECORATIVE
CHAIN

DROP BAR

SLID. DOORS

1'-4" 1'-10 1/8" 1 1/4" 1'-10 1/8" 1 1/4"

· ELEVATION ·

SECTION

70

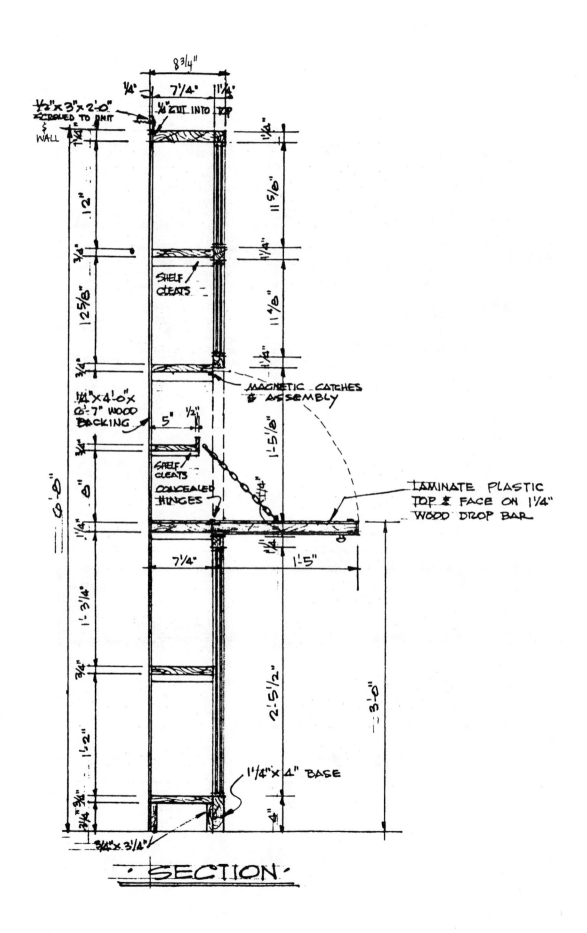

8 3/4"

1/4" 7 1/4" 1 1/4"

1/2" x 3" x 2'-0"
SCREWED TO UNIT

1/8" CUT INTO TOP

1/4"

WALL

1/4"

1 1/4"

12"

11 5/8"

3/4"

1/4"

SHELF
CLEATS

12 5/8"

11 1/8"

3/4"

1/4"

MAGNETIC CATCHES
ASSEMBLY

1 1/4" x 4'-0" x
0'-7" WOOD
BACKING

5" 1/2"

3/4"

SHELF
CLEATS

1'-5 1/8"

6'-0"

8"

CONCEALED
HINGES

1/4"

LAMINATE PLASTIC
TOP # FACE ON 1 1/4"
WOOD DROP BAR

1 1/4"

1/4"

7 1/4"

1'-5"

1'-3 1/4"

2'-5 1/2"

3'-0"

3/4"

1'-2"

1 1/4" x 4" BASE

3/4" 3/4"

4"

3/4" x 3 3/4"

· SECTION ·

71

MATERIAL LIST

2 — 1¼" x 6'-6¾" x 7¼" OUTSIDE ENDS
1 — 1¼" x 4'-0" x 7¼" TOP
1 — 1¼" x 3'-9½" x 4" BASE
4 — ¾" x 7¼" x 3'-9½" SHELVING
1 — ¾" x 5" x 3'-9½" BAR SHELF
1 — ½" x 1½" x 3'-9½" " " FRONT RAIL
1 — 1¼" x 2'-0" x 3'-9" DROP BAR (CUT AT CAB. 7¼")
   1¼" x 1¼" x 1¼" - 36 LIN. FEET
   ¼" x 4'-0" x 4'-0" CUT TO FIT SLID. DOOR OPENINGS
   ¼" x 4'-0" x 6'-0½" BACK PANEL
   ¾" x ¾" x 2'-0" LIN. FEET (DOOR PULLS)
   ½" x 2'-0" DECORATIVE CHAIN
2   MAGNETIC CATCHES
2   HINGES (CONCEALED TYPE)
   ⅜" x 1¼" x 8 LIN. FEET SHELF CLEATS
   1³/₁₆" x ½" x 12 LIN. FEET TOP PREGROOVED TRACK
   1³/₁₆" x ⅜" x " " " BOTTOM " "
2   ¾" x ¾" x 3'-9½" BOTTOM NAILERS
   ½" x 3" x 2'-0" TOP PIECE TO SECURE CAB. TO WALL

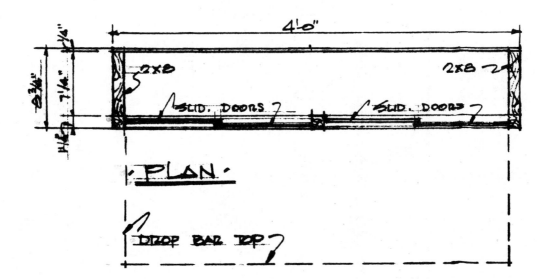

· PLAN ·

DROP BAR TOP

20.

BEVERAGE-SERVICE DUET
A real, old-fashioned, foot-on-the-rail bar

Entertaining's easy when a bar is set up, ready to serve guests in the family room, basement, hobby room, den, or wherever hospitality is dispensed.

This one is a build-it-yourself project for home handymen. The back bar cabinet has mirrored center section and shelves for glasses. Back of bar includes a wine rack. Front of bar has a foot rest. Note useful drawers and cabinets for silver, napkins, serving dishes, bottles, snacks and other aids.

Bar and cabinet are both 6 feet wide; cabinet is 8 feet high; bar is 3 feet, 4 inches high.

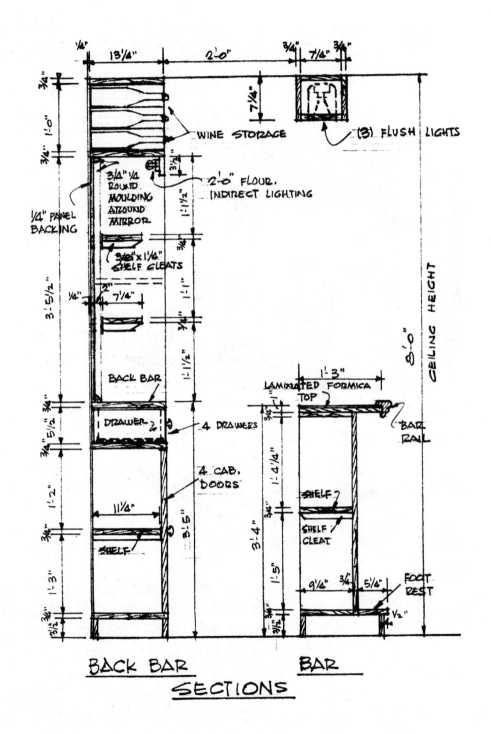

1/4" 13 1/4" 2'-0" 3/4" 7 1/4" 3/4"

3/4"

3/4" 1'-0"

7 1/4"

WINE STORAGE

(3) FLUSH LIGHTS

3/4"

3/4" 1/4 ROUND MOULDING AROUND MIRROR

3 1/2"

2'-0" FLOUR. INDIRECT LIGHTING

1/4" PANEL BACKING

1'-1 1/2"

3/4"

3/8" x 1 1/4" SHELF CLEATS

3'-5 1/2"

1/4" 2" 7 1/4"

1'-1"

3/4"

1'-1 1/2"

BACK BAR

LAMINATED FORMICA TOP

1'-3"

8'-0" CEILING HEIGHT

3/4"

3/4" 5 1/2"

DRAWER

4 DRAWERS

3/4"

1'-4 1/4"

BAR RAIL

3/4"

4 CAB. DOORS

SHELF

1'-2"

11 1/4"

3'-5

3'-4

SHELF CLEAT

3/4"

SHELF

1'-5

1'-3"

9 1/4" 3/4" 5 1/4"

FOOT REST

3/4"

3/4" 3 1/2"

1/2"

3 1/2"

BACK BAR   BAR

SECTIONS

74

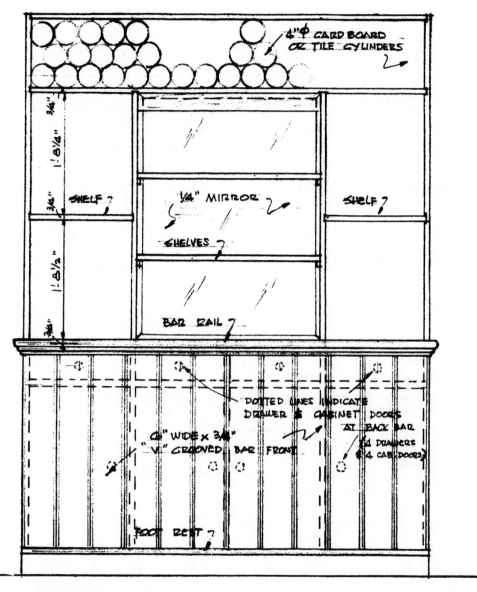

4"⌀ CARD BOARD OR TILE CYLINDERS

¾"

1' 8¼"

¾"

SHELF

¼" MIRROR

SHELVES

SHELF

1' 8½"

¾"

BAR RAIL

DOTTED LINES INDICATE DRAWER & CABINET DOORS AT BACK BAR (11 DRAWERS & 4 CAB DOORS)

6" WIDE x ¾" "V" GROOVED BAR FRONT

FOOT REST

ELEVATION

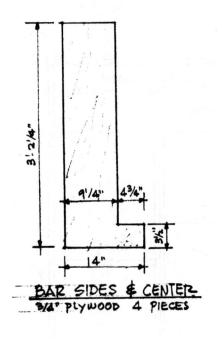

BAR SIDES & CENTER
3/4" PLYWOOD 4 PIECES

Dimensions on bar sides & center: 3'-2 1/4" (height), 9 1/4", 4 3/4", 5 1/2", 14"

MATERIAL LIST:

BACK BAR

Qty	Unit	Description
64	LIN. FT.	3/4" x 13 1/4"
30	LIN. FT	3/4" x 7 1/4"
15	LIN. FT	3/4" x 3 1/2"
1	MIRROR	1/4" x 3'-5" x 2'-8 1/2"
13	LIN. FT	3/4"- 1/4" MOULDING
20	LIN. FT	3/4" x 5 1/4" DRAWERS
1	PLYWOOD	1/4" x 13" x 6'-0" DRAWER BOTTOMS
1	PLYWOOD	3/4" x 2'-5" x 6'-0" CAB DOORS (CUT TO FIT)
1		3/4" x 11 1/4" x 6'-0" " SHELF
1		3/8" x 1 1/4" x 10' SHELF CLEATS
8	DRAWER	KNOBS
4	PAIR	CONCEALED HINGES
1		1/4" x 6'-0" x 8" BACK PANEL

BAR

Qty	Unit	Description
4	PLYWOOD	3/4" x 14" x 5'-2 1/4" CUT FOR BAR SIDES & CENTER
2		3/4" x 3 1/2" x 6'-0"
1		3/4" x 5 1/4" x 6'-0"
18	LIN. FT.	3/4" x 9 1/4"
18	SQ. FT.	3/4" x 6" "V" GROOVED BAR FRONT
1	PLYWOOD	3/4" x 1'-3" x 6'-0" BAR TOP
1	FORMICA	" x " x " " "
1		6'-0" BAR RAIL

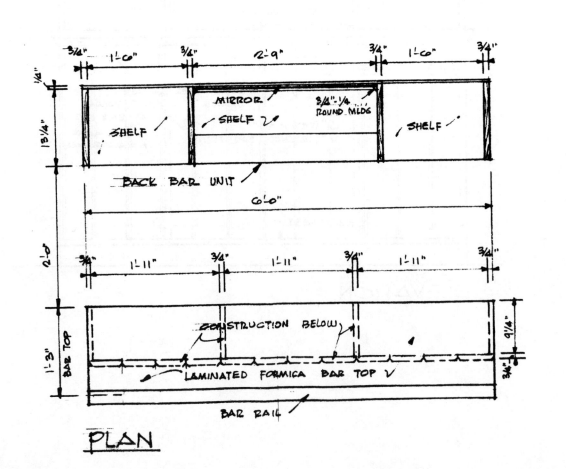

PLAN

21

RECREATION ROOM CORNER

Bar unit with storage features

If your family has entertaining ways, this bar could fit into a corner of family room, recreation room or basement. Cabinets at back store glasses, dishes, soda bottles and refreshments. Below these cabinets, open shelves store bottles and, below them, there is more shelf space. The bar has a foot rest at front and, at back, shelves.

The bar, 3 feet, 5 inches high, projects 6 feet from corner of room to the front.

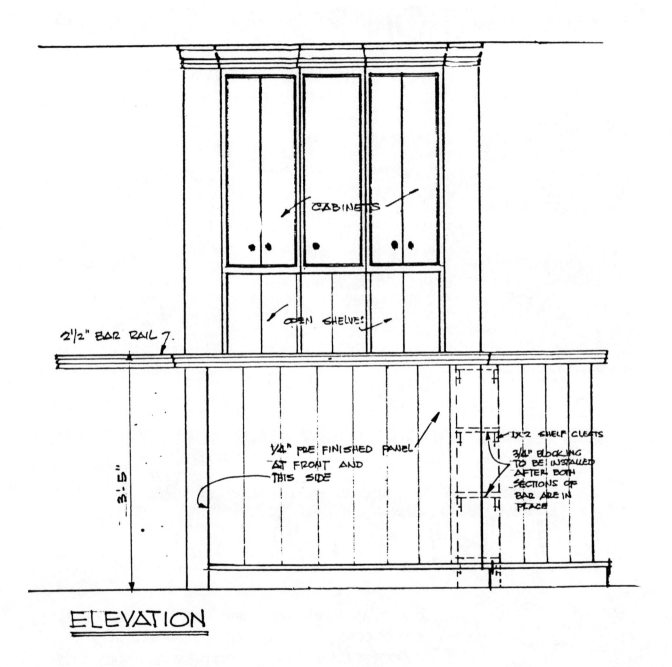

CABINETS

OPEN SHELVES

2¹/₂" BAR RAIL

¼" PRE FINISHED PANEL
AT FRONT AND
THIS SIDE

3'-5"

1X2 SHELF CLEATS

¾" BLOCKING
TO BE INSTALLED
AFTER BOTH
SECTIONS OF
BAR ARE IN
PLACE

ELEVATION

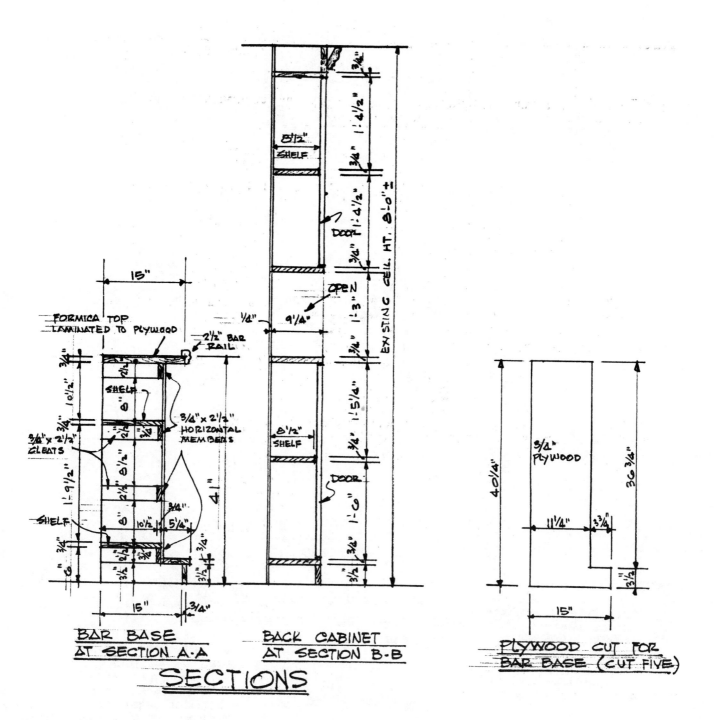

FORMICA TOP
LAMINATED TO PLYWOOD

2½" BAR RAIL

3/4"

SHELF

3/4" x 2½"
HORIZONTAL
MEMBERS

3/8" x 2½"
CLEATS

SHELF

15"

BAR BASE
AT SECTION A·A

8½"
SHELF

DOOR

OPEN

9¼"

8½"
SHELF

DOOR

EXISTING CEIL. HT. 8'-0"±

BACK CABINET
AT SECTION B-B

SECTIONS

3/4"
PLYWOOD

11¼"   3¾"

4'-0¼"

36¾"

3½"

15"

PLYWOOD CUT FOR
BAR BASE (CUT FIVE)

MATERIAL LIST

BAR UNIT

AMT.	SIZE	LOCATION
10 LIN. FT.	3/4" x 15"	BAR TOP
16 " "	3/4" x 15"	BASE SIDES
24 " "	3/4" x 2½"	SHELF CLEATS & HORIZ. FRONT
7 " "	3/4" x 5¼"	TOP FOOT REST
7 " "	3/4" x 3½"	FRONT PIECE FOOT REST
9 " "	¼" x 3'-0"	PRE-FINISHED PANEL, BAR FRONT
14 " "	3/4" x 11¼"	SHELVING

BACK BAR CABINET

AMT.	SIZE	LOCATION
48 LIN. FT.	3/4" x 9¼"	SIDES & SHELVES
8 " "	3/4" x 8½"	INTERMEDIATE SHELVES
6 PIECES	3/4" x 1'-5" x 1'-5"	CORNER SHELVES (CUT)
9 LIN. FT.	3/4" x 1½"	CORNER SHELF CLEATS
1 PIECE	3/4" x 4' x 6'	PLYWOOD DOORS (CUT)
12 PAIR		CONCEALED HINGES
10		KNOBS
10		MAGNETIC CATCHES
5 LIN FT	3/4" x HEIGHT	TOP NAILER
5 " "	3/4" x 4"	CEILING MOULDING
5 " "	3/4" x 3½"	BASE

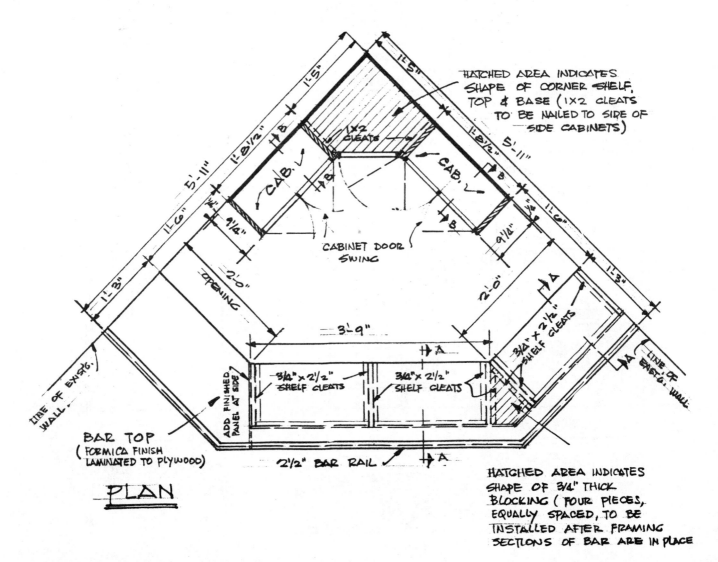

HATCHED AREA INDICATES SHAPE OF CORNER SHELF, TOP & BASE (1x2 CLEATS TO BE NAILED TO SIDE OF SIDE CABINETS)

1x2 CLEATS

CAB.

CAB.

CABINET DOOR SWING

3/4" x 2½" SHELF CLEATS

3/4" x 2½" SHELF CLEATS

3/4" x 2½" SHELF CLEATS

LINE OF EXISTG. WALL

LINE OF EXISTG. WALL

OPENING

ADD FINISHED PANEL AT SIDE

BAR TOP (FORMICA FINISH LAMINATED TO PLYWOOD)

2½" BAR RAIL

PLAN

HATCHED AREA INDICATES SHAPE OF 3/4" THICK BLOCKING (FOUR PIECES, EQUALLY SPACED, TO BE INSTALLED AFTER FRAMING SECTIONS OF BAR ARE IN PLACE

CORNER REFRESHMENT CENTER

FIREPLACES & WOODBINS

22.

FIELDSTONE WITH DOUBLE-WALL FIREBOX

Fireplace circulates warm air around room

Is heating your home a problem? This unique fireplace can help. Double-wall firebox that surrounds fire heats cool air drawn in through outlets at floor level (see drawing). When warm air rises, it is returned to room through warm air outlets (see drawing). Outlets can be extended to grilles in adjoining rooms. Fireplace (6'8" wide, 2'8" deep, 8' high) is brick or stone. Use concrete block finished with stucco for economical exterior.

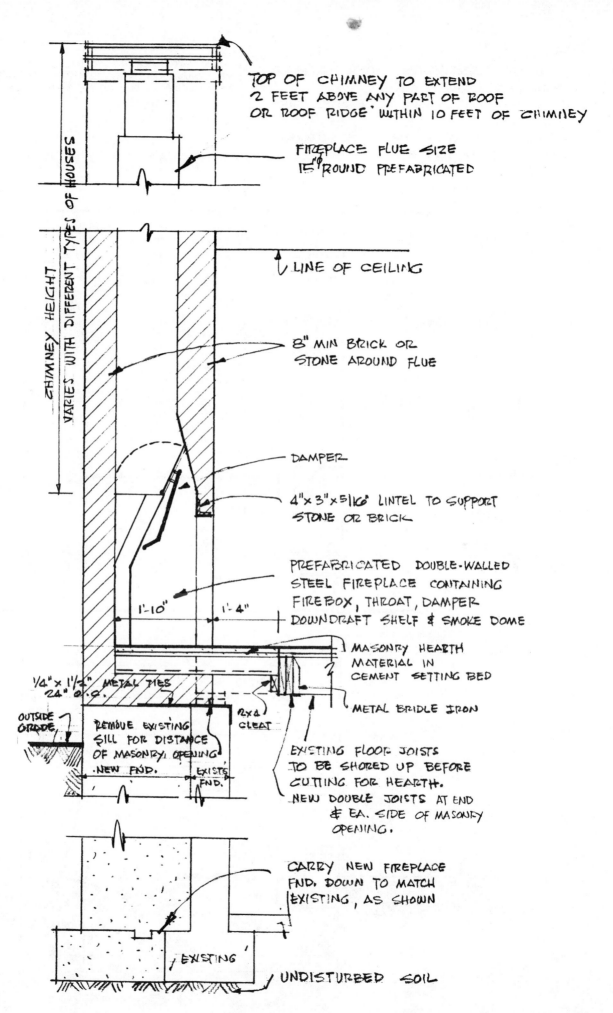

TOP OF CHIMNEY TO EXTEND
2 FEET ABOVE ANY PART OF ROOF
OR ROOF RIDGE WITHIN 10 FEET OF CHIMNEY

FIREPLACE FLUE SIZE
15" ROUND PREFABRICATED

CHIMNEY HEIGHT
VARIES WITH DIFFERENT TYPES OF HOUSES

LINE OF CEILING

8" MIN BRICK OR
STONE AROUND FLUE

DAMPER

4" x 3" x 5/16" LINTEL TO SUPPORT
STONE OR BRICK

PREFABRICATED DOUBLE-WALLED
STEEL FIREPLACE CONTAINING
FIREBOX, THROAT, DAMPER
DOWNDRAFT SHELF & SMOKE DOME

1'-10"   1'-4"

MASONRY HEARTH
MATERIAL IN
CEMENT SETTING BED

1/4" x 1 1/2" METAL TIES
24" O.C.

METAL BRIDLE IRON

OUTSIDE
GRADE

REMOVE EXISTING
SILL FOR DISTANCE
OF MASONRY OPENING
NEW FND.   EXISTG
FND.

2 x 4
CLEAT

EXISTING FLOOR JOISTS
TO BE SHORED UP BEFORE
CUTTING FOR HEARTH.
NEW DOUBLE JOISTS AT END
& EA. SIDE OF MASONRY
OPENING.

CARRY NEW FIREPLACE
FND. DOWN TO MATCH
EXISTING, AS SHOWN

EXISTING

UNDISTURBED SOIL

MATERIAL LIST

- STANDARD DOUBLE-WALLED STEEL FIREPLACE WIDTH 48" × 32" HEIGHT.
- 15" ROUND FLUE, HEIGHT TO BE DETERMINED AT JOB.
- 39 SQ. FT. OF STONE OR BRICK (4" THICK) FOR FIREPLACE FACING.

NOTE:
EXACT AMOUNT OF CONCRETE OR MASONRY UNITS NEEDED FOR FOUNDATION VARIES WITH TYPE OF HOUSE & SITE CONDITIONS.... THIS CAN BE COMPUTED BY CONTRACTOR OR SUPPLIER.

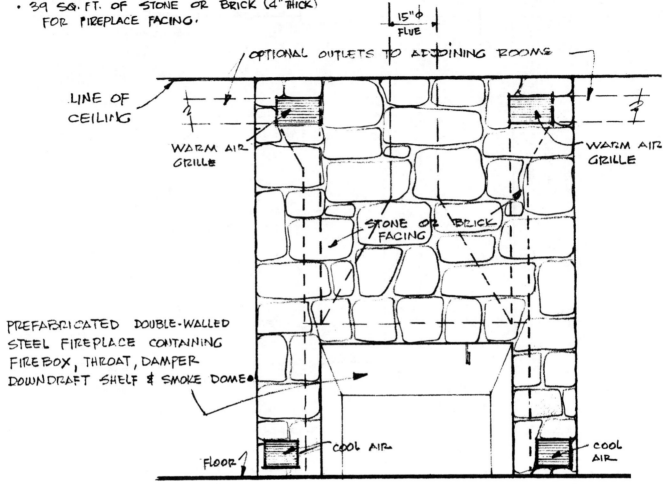

15"∅ FLUE

OPTIONAL OUTLETS TO ADJOINING ROOMS

LINE OF CEILING

WARM AIR GRILLE

WARM AIR GRILLE

STONE OR BRICK FACING

PREFABRICATED DOUBLE-WALLED STEEL FIREPLACE CONTAINING FIREBOX, THROAT, DAMPER DOWNDRAFT SHELF & SMOKE DOME.

COOL AIR

COOL AIR

FLOOR

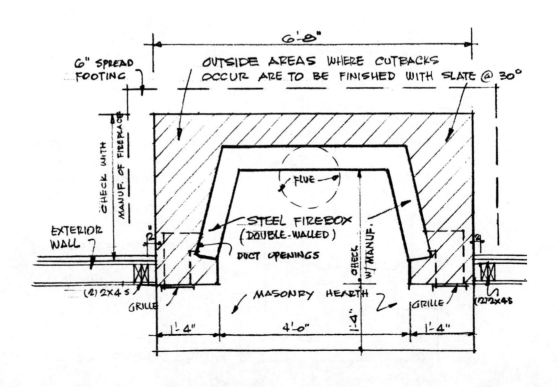

6'-8"

6" SPREAD FOOTING

OUTSIDE AREAS WHERE CUTBACKS OCCUR ARE TO BE FINISHED WITH SLATE @ 30°

CHECK WITH MANUF. OF FIREPLACE

FLUE

EXTERIOR WALL

STEEL FIREBOX (DOUBLE-WALLED)

DUCT OPENINGS

CHECK W/ MANUF.

MASONRY HEARTH

(2) 2×4's

GRILLE

GRILLE

(1) 2×4's

1'-4"

4'-0"

1'-4"

23

CONTEMPORARY SIMPLICITY

A cozy addition to the living room

If you want to give your living room cozy charm, add a fireplace. This one can be centered on a wall or built into a corner. It can be added to an outside wall with a minimum amount of alteration work. The wood mantel extends full width over fireplace and wood box. Use brick or stone to face the fireplace; 4-inch firebrick to line the inside. Fireplace is 9 feet, 6 inches wide; 2 feet, 5 inches deep.

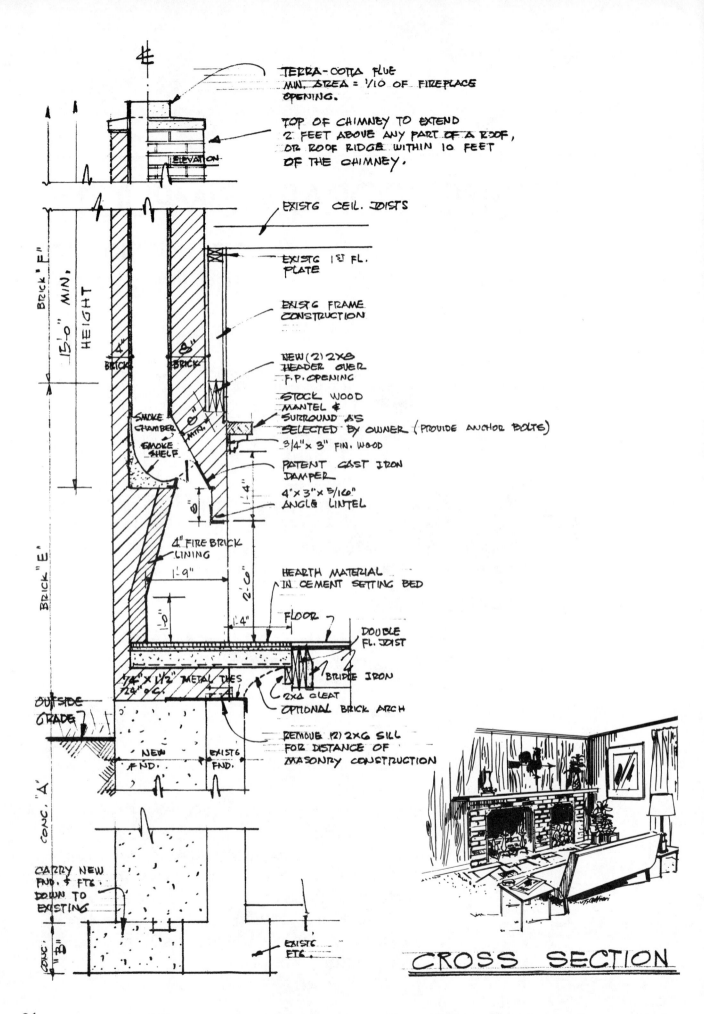

TERRA-COTTA FLUE
MIN. AREA = 1/10 OF FIREPLACE
OPENING.

TOP OF CHIMNEY TO EXTEND
2 FEET ABOVE ANY PART OF A ROOF,
OR ROOF RIDGE WITHIN 10 FEET
OF THE CHIMNEY.

ELEVATION

EXIST'G CEIL. JOISTS

EXIST'G 1ST FL. PLATE

EXIST'G FRAME CONSTRUCTION

NEW (2) 2x8 HEADER OVER F.P. OPENING

STOCK WOOD MANTEL & SURROUND AS SELECTED BY OWNER (PROVIDE ANCHOR BOLTS)

3/4" x 3" FIN. WOOD

PATENT CAST IRON DAMPER

4" x 3" x 5/16" ANGLE LINTEL

BRICK "F"

15'-0" MIN. HEIGHT

4" BRICK

8" BRICK

SMOKE CHAMBER

SMOKE SHELF

4" FIRE BRICK LINING

BRICK "E"

1'-9"

2'-0"

1'-0"

HEARTH MATERIAL IN CEMENT SETTING BED

FLOOR

1'-4"

DOUBLE FL. JOIST

BRIDGE IRON

2x4 CLEAT

OPTIONAL BRICK ARCH

1/4" x 1 1/2" METAL TIES 24" O.C.

OUTSIDE GRADE

NEW FND.

EXIST'G FND.

REMOVE (2) 2x6 SILL FOR DISTANCE OF MASONRY CONSTRUCTION

CONC. "A"

CARRY NEW FND. & FTG. DOWN TO EXISTING

CONC. "B"

EXIST'G FTG.

CROSS SECTION

MATERIAL LIST

CONCRETE

"A" 19 SQ. FT. X DEPTH (MEASURED IN FEET TO FOOTING) FOR SQ. FT. OF REQ. CONC.

"B" + 26 SQ. FT. OF CONC. FOR FOOTING.

BRICK

"D" 22 SQ. FT. OF FACE BRICK FOR INSIDE (OR STONE)

"E" 77 SQ. FT. OF OF BRICK FOR BOTTOM SECTION FROM FLOOR UP TO & INCL. SMOKE CHAMBER

"F" + 3.5 SQ. FT. X HEIGHT, IN FEET, FOR TOTAL BRICK REQ. IN HEIGHT.

FLUE

8½" X 13" TERRA COTTA FLUE, FOR 15'-0" HEIGHT (8 - 2'-0" SECTIONS ARE REQUIRED)

STEEL ANGLES

(2) 4" X 3" X 5/16" LINTELS OVER FIREPLACE & WOOD BOX.

DAMPER SIZE = 52½" LENGTH X 9⅞" WIDTH

WOOD MANTEL

3" X 6" FINISHED, 10'-6" LONG.

(4) 3" X 3" WOOD BRACKETS

(1) 3/4" X 3" BOARD BEHIND BRACKETS

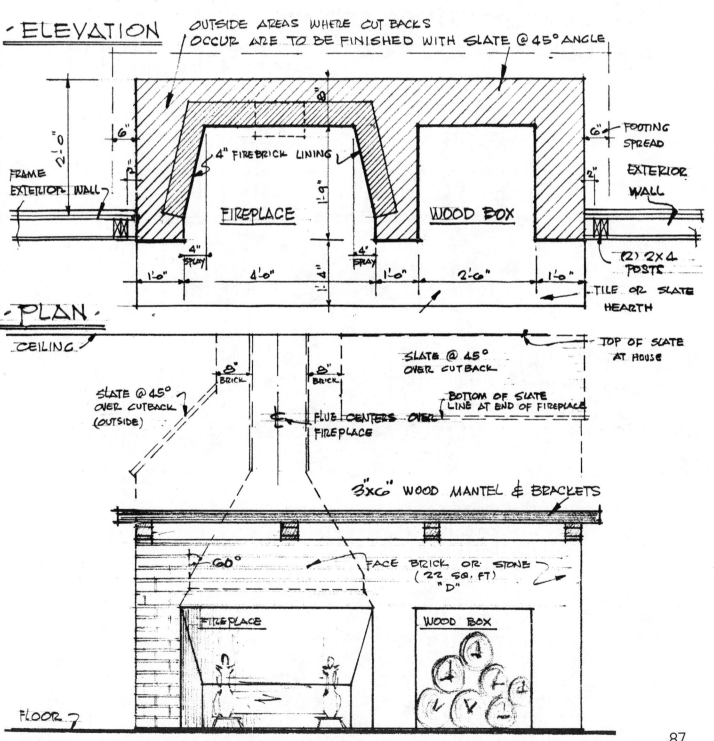

· ELEVATION ·

OUTSIDE AREAS WHERE CUT BACKS OCCUR ARE TO BE FINISHED WITH SLATE @ 45° ANGLE

4" FIREBRICK LINING

FRAME EXTERIOR WALL

FIREPLACE

1'-9"

WOOD BOX

6" FOOTING SPREAD

EXTERIOR WALL

2"

(2) 2 X 4 POSTS

TILE OR SLATE HEARTH

4" SPLAY

4" SPLAY

1'-0"   4'-0"   1'-0"   2'-6"   1'-0"

· PLAN ·

CEILING

SLATE @ 45° OVER CUTBACK (OUTSIDE)

8" BRICK

8" BRICK

SLATE @ 45° OVER CUTBACK

FLUE CENTERS OVER FIREPLACE

BOTTOM OF SLATE LINE AT END OF FIREPLACE

TOP OF SLATE AT HOUSE

3" X 6" WOOD MANTEL & BRACKETS

60°

FACE BRICK OR STONE (22 SQ. FT.) "D"

FIREPLACE

WOOD BOX

FLOOR

24.

COLONIAL WITH DECORATIVE STORAGE

Plan includes storage cabinet and built-in wood box

A fireplace not only contributes to your enjoyment but to the value of your home. This one with its built-in woodbox can be added along any outside wall. It is 13 feet, 3½ inches wide with the storage cabinet; 10 feet wide without it. The decorative cabinet has open shelves above; a closed storage unit below. Brick or stone is suggested for the facing material, with 4-inch firebrick lining. The fireplace is 2 feet, 5 inches deep; height to the mantel is 4 feet, 6 inches.

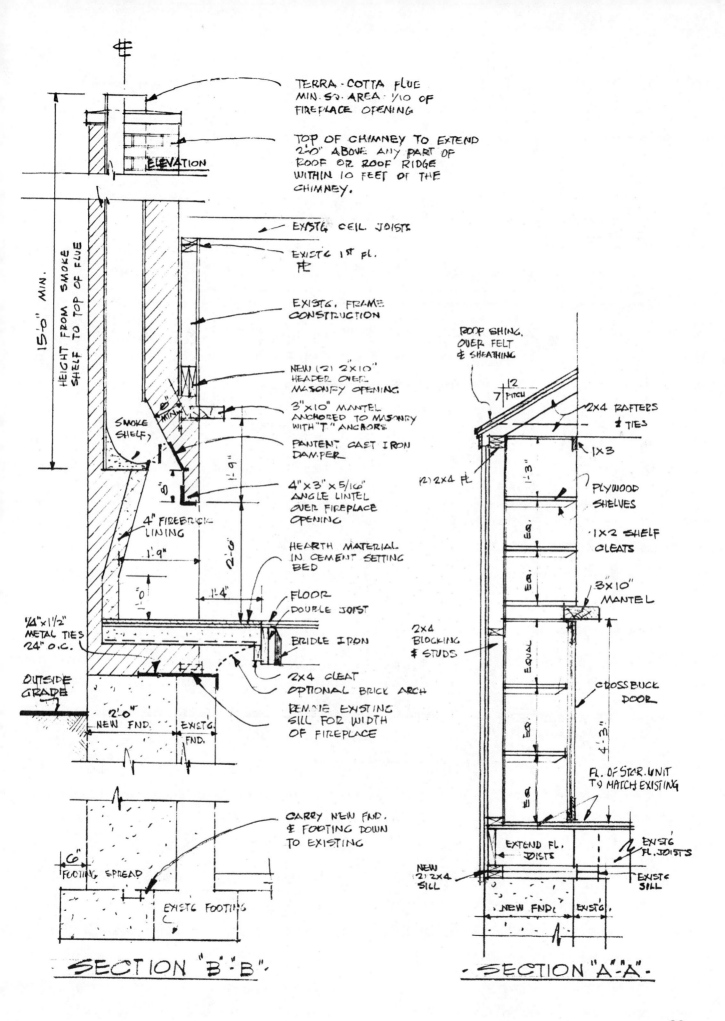

ELEVATION

TERRA-COTTA FLUE
MIN. SQ. AREA 1/10 OF
FIREPLACE OPENING

TOP OF CHIMNEY TO EXTEND
2'-0" ABOVE ANY PART OF
ROOF OR ROOF RIDGE
WITHIN 10 FEET OF THE
CHIMNEY.

EXISTG. CEIL. JOISTS

EXISTG. 1ST FL. FL.

EXISTG. FRAME
CONSTRUCTION

NEW (2) 2"x10"
HEADER OVER
MASONRY OPENING

3"x10" MANTEL
ANCHORED TO MASONRY
WITH "T" ANCHORS

PATENT CAST IRON
DAMPER

4"x3"x5/16"
ANGLE LINTEL
OVER FIREPLACE
OPENING

HEARTH MATERIAL
IN CEMENT SETTING
BED

FLOOR
DOUBLE JOIST

BRIDLE IRON

2x4 CLEAT
OPTIONAL BRICK ARCH

REMOVE EXISTING
SILL FOR WIDTH
OF FIREPLACE

15'-0" MIN.
HEIGHT FROM SMOKE SHELF TO TOP OF FLUE

SMOKE
SHELF

6" MIN.

4" FIREBRICK
LINING

1'-9"

2'-0"

1'-4"

1'-9"

1/4"x1 1/2"
METAL TIES
24" O.C.

OUTSIDE
GRADE

2'-0"
NEW FND.   EXISTG.
FND.

CARRY NEW FND.
& FOOTING DOWN
TO EXISTING

6"
FOOTING SPREAD

EXISTG FOOTING

SECTION "B"-"B"

ROOF SHING.
OVER FELT
& SHEATHING

12
7 PITCH

2x4 RAFTERS
& TIES

1x3

(2) 2x4 PL.

1'-3"

PLYWOOD
SHELVES

1x2 SHELF
CLEATS

3x10"
MANTEL

2x4
BLOCKING
& STUDS

EQUAL

CROSSBUCK
DOOR

4'-3"

FL. OF STOR. UNIT
TO MATCH EXISTING

EXTEND FL.
JOISTS

EXISTG
FL. JOISTS

NEW
(2) 2x4
SILL

EXISTG
SILL

NEW FND.   EXISTG.

SECTION "A"-"A"

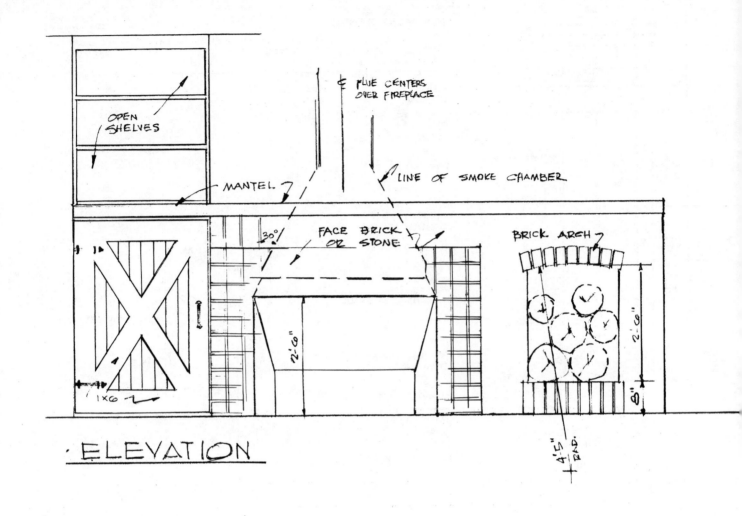

OPEN
SHELVES

MANTEL

₵ FLUE CENTERS
OVER FIREPLACE

LINE OF SMOKE CHAMBER

FACE BRICK
OR STONE

BRICK ARCH

30°

1x6

2'-0"

2'-0"

8"

4'-5"
RAD.

ELEVATION

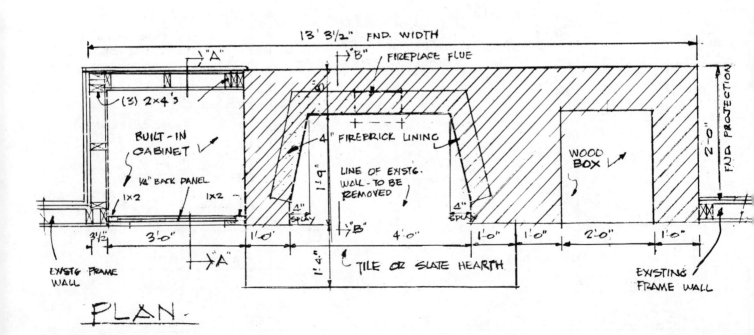

13' 3½" FND. WIDTH

"A"

"B" FIREPLACE FLUE

(3) 2x4's

BUILT-IN
CABINET

¼" BACK PANEL

1x2   1x2

4" FIREBRICK LINING

LINE OF EXISTG.
WALL - TO BE
REMOVED

4"
SPLAY

4"
SPLAY

WOOD
BOX

2'-0"
FND. PROJECTION

EXISTG. FRAME
WALL

3½"   3'-0"   1'-0"

"A"

"B"

1'-4"

4'-0"

TILE OR SLATE HEARTH

1'-0"   1'-0"   2'-0"   1'-0"

1'-9"

EXISTING
FRAME WALL

PLAN.

NO-MASONRY PREFAB

Easy to install with zero-clearance; flanked with bookshelves and a hidden log-box

The beauty of this design is that it can easily be adapted to existing conditions because no foundation is required. The firebox is pre-fabricated type that can be built directly onto a wood floor by following the manufacturer's specs for fireproofing. The flue pipe is enclosed in the wood chase. Bookshelves flank the brick-faced firebox. The unit sits two feet out from the existing room wall to allow wood storage behind the bookcases. The total, finished unit is 2-feet deep, 8-feet 5-inches wide, and the height of the room.

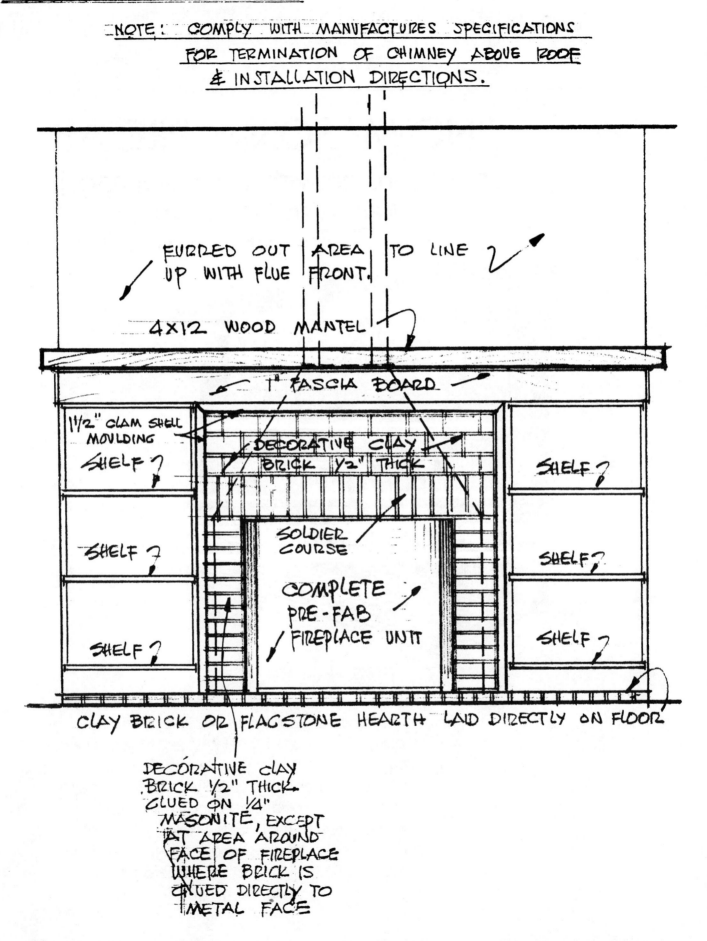

· FRONT ELEVATION ·

NOTE: COMPLY WITH MANUFACTURES SPECIFICATIONS
FOR TERMINATION OF CHIMNEY ABOVE ROOF
& INSTALLATION DIRECTIONS.

FURRED OUT AREA TO LINE
UP WITH FLUE FRONT.

4X12 WOOD MANTEL

1" FASCIA BOARD

1½" CLAM SHELL MOULDING
SHELF?

DECORATIVE CLAY
BRICK ½" THICK

SHELF?

SHELF?

SOLDIER COURSE

SHELF?

COMPLETE PRE-FAB FIREPLACE UNIT

SHELF?

SHELF?

CLAY BRICK OR FLAGSTONE HEARTH LAID DIRECTLY ON FLOOR

DECORATIVE CLAY
BRICK ½" THICK.
GLUED ON ¼"
MASONITE, EXCEPT
AT AREA AROUND
FACE OF FIREPLACE
WHERE BRICK IS
GLUED DIRECTLY TO
METAL FACE

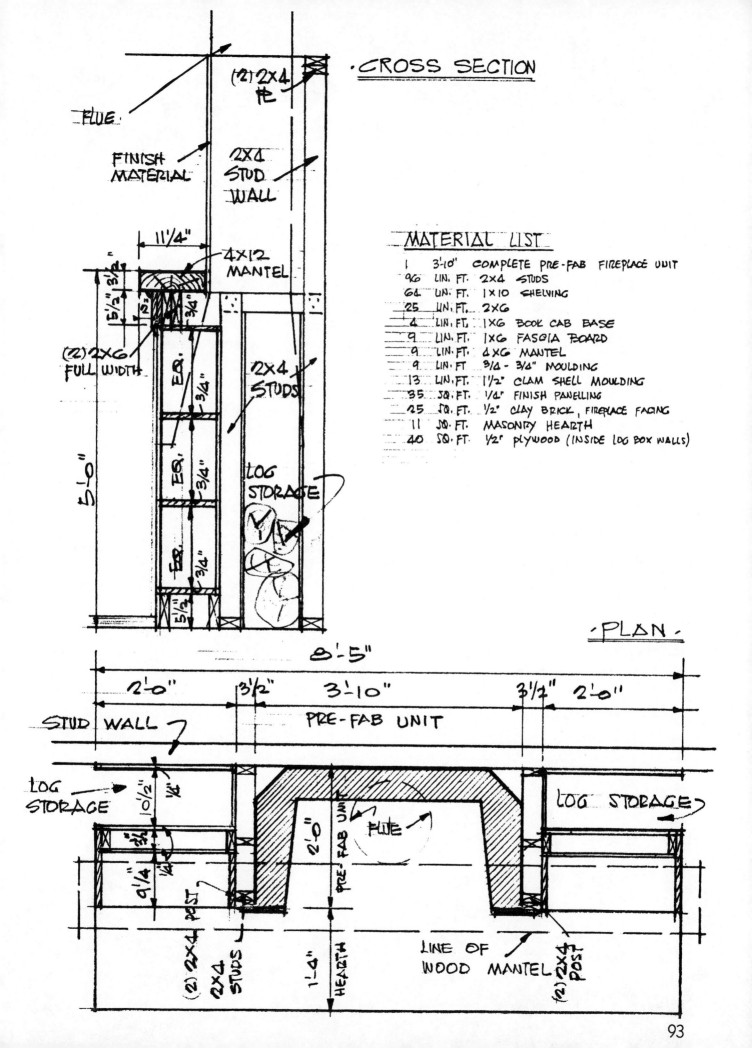

· CROSS SECTION ·

FLUE

FINISH MATERIAL

(2) 2×4 R.

2×4 STUD WALL

4×12 MANTEL

11 1/4"

(2) 2×6 FULL WIDTH

2×4 STUDS

LOG STORAGE

EQ. 3/4"

EQ. 3/4"

EQ. 3/4"

5'-0"

MATERIAL LIST

1		3'-10"	COMPLETE PRE-FAB FIREPLACE UNIT
96	LIN. FT.	2×4	STUDS
64	LIN. FT.	1×10	SHELVING
25	LIN. FT.	2×6	
4	LIN. FT.	1×6	BOOK CAB BASE
9	LIN. FT.	1×6	FASGIA BOARD
9	LIN. FT.	4×6	MANTEL
9	LIN. FT.	3/4 - 3/4"	MOULDING
13	LIN. FT.	1 1/2"	CLAM SHELL MOULDING
35	SQ. FT.	1/4"	FINISH PANELLING
25	SQ. FT.	1/2"	CLAY BRICK, FIREPLACE FACING
11	SQ. FT.		MASONRY HEARTH
40	SQ. FT.	1/2"	PLYWOOD (INSIDE LOG BOX WALLS)

· PLAN ·

8'-5"

2'-0" | 3 1/2" | 3'-10" | 3 1/2" | 2'-0"

STUD WALL | PRE-FAB UNIT

LOG STORAGE

FLUE

PRE-FAB UNIT

2'-0"

LOG STORAGE

(2) 2×4 POST

2×4 STUDS

1'-4" HEARTH

LINE OF WOOD MANTEL

(2) 2×4 POST